THE FIRST LIAR NEVER
HAS A CHANCE

Published by Crown Publishers, Inc., 201 East 50th Street, New
York, New York 10022. Member of the Crown Publishing
Group.

Random House, Inc. New York, Toronto, London, Sydney,
Auckland

CROWN and colophon are trademarks of Crown Publishers,
Inc.

Manufactured in the United States of America

Library of Congress Cataloging-in-Publication Data
Garry, Jim.
    The first liar never has a chance : Curly, Jack and Bill (&
other characters of the hills, brush and plains) / Jim
Garry.—1st ed.
        p.   cm.—(The Library of the American West)
    Includes index.
    1. West (U.S.)—Social life and customs—Anecdotes.   2.
Folklore—West (U.S.)   I. Title.   II. Series.
F596.G37   1994
978—dc20   94-4781
                                                        CIP

ISBN 0-517-58815-3

10 9 8 7 6 5 4 3 2 1

First Edition

To all the old-timers,
from Brushy Creek to Powder River,
who have told me stories and shown me the Land.

Contents

+≡◈≡◈≡+

ACKNOWLEDGMENTS

For every story in this book there are a couple of dozen that aren't in print but were necessary to hear to feel the flow of the river of tradition that these were dipped from. I want to thank all those who shared their tales with me.

Grace Mary, my favorite sister, is the main person responsible for helping me figure out how to translate spoken language into written language. Herman Viola and Stephen Topping kept encouraging or threatening me, as needed, to get this book finished. Earl and Ethel Throne provided me with a hideout for my writing. The good folks at Sheridan Office Services, Shari Peddicord and Debbie Dudrey, helped to get the manscript in legible form. Sandy Nykerk was gracious enough to take the jacket photo and skillful enough to make me look better than I do.

To all of you who helped, whether it was working with me on the book or just sharing your stories with me, thank you.

These tales are not creations of mine. They belong to the
soil and to the people of the soil. Like all things that
belong, they have their roots deep in the place of their being,
deep in the past. They are an outgrowth; they embody
the geniuses of divergent races and peoples who even while
fiercely opposing each other blended their traditions.
However all this may be, the tales are just tales. As tales I
have listened to them in camps under stars and on ranch
galleries out in the brush. As tales, without any ethnological
palaver, I have tried to set them down.

J. Frank Dobie,
from the introduction to
CORONADO'S CHILDREN

THE FIRST LIAR NEVER
HAS A CHANCE

There was no sense in going to the garden until late, so we sat around a big plate of cookies, a coffeepot, and, for me in my pre-coffee-drinking days, a pitcher of milk. There was no thought of turning on the radio or TV; Annie and Vic were the entertainment.

About nine-thirty or ten, when we were running desperately low on cookies and I had laughed as much as I could stand, we figured it had been dark long enough for the coons to get active. Vic had headlights for us to wear, so the two of us adjourned to the garden, accoutred like miners going to war. I had my little single-shot .410, a half dozen shells in my pocket, and my varmint call hanging around my neck. Vic had a 12-gauge automatic that was pretty nearly as long as he was tall and a bandolier of shells over his shoulder like a cartoon Mexican bandit. We ignored Annie's laughter as we crossed the driveway and yard to the garden. We sat down, back to back, along the edge of the garden facing the creek, and I explained to Vic how the hunt would, in theory, develop.

"We'll just sit here quietly for a few minutes. Then I'll start to call. Keep your lamp pointed up so that only a little light will reach the ground. That will be enough to pick up eyes. If you see something, whisper to me. When you're ready to shoot, I'll turn my head and put my light on the animal. That'll freeze him for a second or two and you can shoot."

The garden was level with the house, but beyond that the ground sloped away in pasture down to the brush along Boggy a couple of hundred yards away. There was a fence line about halfway, separating Annie and Vic's land from the neighbor's. We sat quietly, knowing all this was there, though we couldn't see it. We passed half an hour in silence, then I began to call. After about another half hour, Vic whis-

3

pered that he could see eyes moving up toward us from the creek. I told him to stay still and just watch the eyes. I called again and Vic said the coon was in range. I turned and dropped my light beam along the barrel of Vic's shotgun. When you are fifteen or sixteen years old, you haven't figured out yet that as people get older—Vic was probably past seventy by then—night vision isn't what it used to be. It took only a couple of seconds for me to realize that the eyes we were looking at, though apparently at ground level, were attached to a cow back across the fence and not to a coon just outside the garden. My remark that he probably shouldn't shoot it was drowned by the roar of his 12-gauge.

The blessing of advancing years is that it affects hearing as well as vision. The shotgun blast deafened Vic for a few seconds, so he couldn't hear the sound of a cow boring a hole successively through the brush, the creek, then more brush. I was sitting, just slightly awestruck, unable to speak, telling myself that, at that range, the shot would not have been fatal, but that we could have a blind cow to explain to whoever had just leased the neighboring pasture. Before I could speak, Annie called from the house.

"How many of you are left?"

"I got it," Vic replied triumphantly. To me he said, "Leave it there. If that's the path they're using to come to the garden, any others will stay away rather than go over the dead one. I don't want to shoot any more unless I have to." Being thankful for Vic's knowledge of local folklore, I agreed and we returned to the house, Vic ebullient for defending his property, I silent, contemplating what to do next. I decided the best thing to do was to sleep on it, so I said my good nights and went home.

The next day I saddled up Miss Kitty and headed cross-country to visit Annie and Vic. I was riding down Boggy, trying to appear casual, when I met the fellow who had just leased the pasture. He was new to the country and I didn't know him except by sight. As we talked, a cow, her face a mass of blisterlike welts, walked out of the brush. We studied her, he in bewilderment, I counting eyes. Surprisingly, he didn't seem to notice the change in my demeanor, the relaxation of my whole being when my count got to two, whole and undamaged. I realized he was talking to me, asking what I thought might have happened to the cow.

"I don't know," I said, feeling suddenly inspired. "Maybe she stuck her head in a yellow jacket nest."

"Looks more like what those big red wasps would do," he replied.

"Could be," I said, made my excuses, and rode on.

As I rode back home, the country opened up. The dread of telling Vic we'd blinded a cow evaporated. As I realized that a difficult dilemma had become a story, other stories began to rise out of the black soil of my homeland. Across the road from Annie and Vic's house, Uncle Tom, Annie's pappa, had turned up an old Spanish spur when he first plowed that field. Their home had been the old, three-room Barker School, where Mamma had taught for several years back during the Depression, years when she was paid with vouchers that could never be honored since the school system was as broke as everyone else. Across that prairie, from Brushy Creek, a couple of miles to the south, all the way to Cottonwood Creek, four miles to the north, the settlers from Bastrop (my ancestors included) and the Comanches fought a running, horseback battle. From high ground I could see the girders of the old Brushy bridge, built after the '21 flood, the flood that had taken out the old bridge and some of Jimbo Grey's family with it. I passed where Uncle Emzy's house had stood, where he and Daddy had stopped so he

5

could get his six-shooter and give driving lessons to a trucker. On the hill across Brushy from our house was the seep, now a tank, where my great-grandfather, a boy himself, had camped when he first came into the country. Every acre of that piece of country had a story. Each of the stories had grown from that soil. My family, and others like them, had come because of the deep, rich, black soil. Here the tallgrass prairie trailed off to drop down to the sandier coastal plains to the south. A few miles to the east were the post oaks, the edge of the great American forest. An equal distance to the west was the Balconies Scarpment, the edge of the short grass prairie. Here, long ago, buffalo wintered. On early maps it was marked as Wild Horse Prairies. Here my family came to run cattle and horses when there were no more buffalo. Here too my family built the railroad, hotels, and the cotton compress in the new town that sprang up around the railroad. Here my family adapted to the changing times and plowed up most of their grasslands for cotton. The stories connected me to the grass-covered prairie of my great-grandparents' day as well as to the cotton fields of my childhood. I had learned the stories simply by living there. I'd absorbed many of them by osmosis. Others I'd learned consciously because I loved them. Still others had been hammered into me whether I wanted to know them or not; they were important to know, someday I'd understand why. As I grew and my horizons expanded, I knew instinctively that every piece of country was like home. There were stories growing from the soil, just as there were plants growing from it. All my life I have been drawn to places where stories live. There I find the storytellers I love, people of place who have blended their native soil into their character and their tales. For the last fifteen years, as a professional storyteller, I have searched out, or stumbled onto and recognized, places where stories grow, where the telling fits into the texture of life so that folks just naturally tell them. When I find stories I can tell, I dig up every version I can find, every piece I can learn, and build a tale I can tell. It's not a great way to make money ... but it beats working. And it keeps me, at least most of the time, in our mythical landscape.

THE
PLACES
WHERE
STORIES
GROW

It is often and rightly said that we need to know our history—to know where we came from and how we got to where we are today. It is equally important to know our mythology—to know who it is we are trying to be. Our history tells us who we are, our myths who we are trying to be. Our country, at its origin, faced a problem. We had severed ourselves from much of the myth of Europe, and we didn't possess the vast stretch of time needed to create a new one. Our ancestors came here to escape their past, to begin again and to create a new world. But they discovered that in doing so they had no past here on which to hang their myths. So we traded the infinite thing we had for the one we didn't. Lacking vast time, we set our myth in vast space. The West became our mythical landscape, the perfect place for the ideal people to develop a great culture.

Since myths must have heroes, we created heroes in our mythical landscape. Originally, they were the explorers who poked through the passes of the Appalachians into the vast forests that stretched from there to the Mississippi. These explorers were hunter-farmers who wielded rifle, axe, and plow to create a new land for their own families and those who followed them. To those who remained in the settled, civilized lands east of the mountains, the deeds of these explorers sounded heroic. There were heroic hardships in the wilderness: isolation, wild animals, endless, backbreaking toil. There were people already there—people who contested these heroes' right to the lands promised to them by their God. When those first hunter-explorers returned with tales of great and fertile lands beyond the mountains, learned men prophesied that it would take a thousand years to settle that vastness. It took little more than a single generation.

The vast, impenetrable forest of the mythical landscape was reduced to woods, the fearsome wild animals reduced to the objects of sport, and the native peoples reduced to troublesome groups to be dealt with, when necessary, by the army. What had been a vast wilderness became a land of farms with towns at the crossroads and cities growing along the major rivers. Domesticated, the land of myth disappeared. We again turned our eyes and our consciousness westward, searching for our myth and ourselves. Texas became the land of the myth in the second quarter of the nineteenth century (it has remained a piece of it since—its size and variety of landscapes have caused some part of it always to fit the mold) but was surpassed by the West Coast in the 1850s. Oregon's and Washington's lush valleys and timber-covered slopes were like the East's only better, so the stories went. California had the lure of King Solomon's mines; gold to be picked up off the ground for anyone not too lazy to bend over. Surprisingly quickly, East Texas and coastal Oregon and Washington were settled and farmed while the easy pickings of the California goldfields gave way to corporate operations where the actual miners were wage earners. The prospectors turned east to the Rockies. Finally, with all the well-watered land spoken for, the country turned collectively to the great arid and semiarid middle of the country. And here, I suspect almost to our surprise, we found the mythological landscape we needed to sustain us. For here everything was cut not just on a larger scale but in a different pattern. Here was a land of mythic dimensions to match our view of ourselves.

The West it was called then. The West, capitalized, it remains. It is a vast dry sea, stretched from the forest on the east to the Sierras and the Cascades on the west (in a few places stretching all the way to the ocean). It spills into Canada on the north and the southern deserts drop deep into Mexico. The Rockies are merely islands in this sea of grass and brush and rocky bare soils. It is a land of little rain, yet clouds often dominate the sky. Here, with no trees to block the view, we watch thunderheads build, see the jet stream whip the tops off into anvils, and witness their power in lightning flashes. When a storm like that descends on us, we wait: for hailstones the size of turkey eggs, tornadoes, winds that flatten crops, floods, or just a few large icy drops and a breeze that cools us for a few minutes before the sun returns to continue baking the already-dry land. Here the animals were unlike those of the forests to the east. The rabbits were huge and sported ears like jackasses'. There were antelope, fleet-footed beyond imagination. Prairie dog towns stretched for miles. The bison, hard to imagine as an individual animal, were incomprehensible in their millions. If a hero needed dragons to slay, there were grizzly bears aplenty. And for the hero's necessary mythic opponent, there was the Indian. From the palisaded cities of earthen mounds along the rivers of the eastern plains to the stone and adobe pueblos in the southwest, from the horse nomads following the bison herds to every variety of hunter-gatherer, farmer, and fisherman, the Indians were, in the minds of the mythmakers, children of a lesser god, contesting our destiny.

Who was the hero of this vast mythical landscape? Who was at home in the great grass sea but still had contact with civilization? The cowboy. We had experimented with a number of heroes in the West and finally decided, for many and diverse reasons, on the cowboy as the standard-bearer. The image of the cowboy was not, of course, the real cowboy. The mythical cowboy was cowboy, lawman, scout, rancher, and knight-errant all rolled into one. He became the image known to the world through art, literature, film, and story: the hard-riding, slow-talking, straight-shooting horseman. He was at home in the western vastness yet he had ties to towns, those oases of civilization in the Wild West; here he kept the soft qualities of civilization balanced with the bedrock hardness of the wild, a necessity in our national culture. In the myth it is he who made the West safe for all those who followed. It is a myth now well settled and universal. The cowboy and the mythical West are known the world over.

While we were creating and peopling our mythical landscape, there were also humans moving into and settling the West. For generations now those of us in the West have inhabited a contradictory place, a timeless piece of country, a land that is nothing more than the floor of the sky, and that is a functioning part of the United States. We talk on the phone, listen to the radio, and watch TV. We drive to town in cars (or pickups), sometimes even on paved roads. Yet there are times, often when we least expect it, that we slide through the crack into that timeless, mythical world. Called there by a cloud (a meadowlark, the slant of the snow, a rock, the sunrise), we are privileged to spend a little while in the limitless world without politics, an economy, or any other problem—the mythical landscape.

We had ridden for a half hour one morning lit by alpenglow as the not-yet-risen sun reflected off the bottom of the cloud above the valley. Now the rising sun struck the dust cloud stirred up by the eighty head of horses we were driving and turned it from gray volcanic ash to a silver vortex. As the crack opened, the cloud released its moisture. The three of us touched spurs to our horses and loped through the crack as the sun's first rays worked the magic of the alchemists on the huge raindrops. I looked back and saw the mountains as the first mammoth hunters had, pristine beyond the imaginings of even the best-intentioned developers. We rode back through the crack at the corrals, but when I looked at Kathy and Don, I knew they had been there too.

"A month's wages," Kathy said, summing up why we live and work here.

"Yeah, but let's not tell Ms. B. that," Don replied, reminding us that we had to live in both worlds. I said nothing, just wondered where in the mythical landscape they had been.

We take living in two worlds in stride for a simple reason: even we whites have been here for a while now; we have some tradition, some history, to leaven the myth. It is a tradition passed down, through stories mostly. The stories are entertainment, but, beyond that, they are the history of this land and its peoples, and they are the lessons of decorum, behavior, and manners that preserve the roots of our cultures, cultures that date back to the Old West.

The Old West could perhaps best be defined as the West

whose people and goods were still moved by animals, primarily horses, mules, and oxen. The last generation of the Old West—those who can remember the first time they rode in a car, talked on a phone, or listened to a radio—is getting old, old unto death. Soon we will have only the stories they told.

I live now in the Powder River Basin, a tattered fringe of the Old West. The journey that has brought me here has been long and interesting: twenty-odd years of searching out the stories of this land some of us call home and others view as only a mythical place. But this journey, like all journeys, began at home. It began with Daddy's stories.

Brushy
Creek
and Beyond

⊹⊱◈⊰⊹

The great blackland prairie stretched down from the last glacial moraines as a great swath of tall grass, able to choke out any tree whose wayward seed fell on its thick mat. It narrowed as it tended southward until, no more than a thin finger, its heavy black soil faded away in Central Texas. Daddy's Grandpa Barker rode into it for the first time as a boy. He was a Texian, born before the Revolution and though still quite young, considered mature enough to take a herd of cattle out onto the unexplored grass sea. Accompanied by a black slave only a couple of years older than himself, he set off from the settlement at Bastrop in search of grazing land. The two boys camped at a seep on the hills south of Brushy Creek. From there they could see, fifteen miles to the east, the edge of the great American forest. Fifteen miles to the west rose the Balconies Scarpment, the edge of the short-grass prairie.

Grandpa Barker and the slave didn't stay all that long on that first trip. One day, while they were in camp, they saw a group of mounted Indians north of Brushy. Prudently, they decided not to wait long enough to determine whether they were friendly Tonkawa or not-so-friendly Comanches. The two of them jumped on the horse they shared and lit out for Bastrop. But Grandpa Barker kept coming back until, by the 1850s, he'd built a house beside Brushy and settled down. For a generation the family grew and prospered (with some time off from prosperity due to selling horses and mules and running cotton to Mexico for Confederate money during the Civil War). With a few other families scattered along the creeks, Grandpa Barker and his clan farmed the bottoms and ran cattle on the vastness of the prairie. They took on the shape of the land. As the tall grass was a transition from the forest to the great buffalo plains, so the people lived with one foot in the Deep South and one in the West.

In the mid-1870s the railroads arrived in Central Texas and, within a few years, enough people arrived to change the blackland. Where before there had been small plowed fields in an immensity of grass, now fields of cotton stretched to the horizon and pastures had to be fenced. Grandpa Barker's four oldest sons, Bob, Frate, Tom, and Rufe, drove the cattle west, hunting unfenced grass. After a few years west of the Pecos, they returned. Bob and Frate stopped up on the 'scarpment near Austin; Tom, and Rufe came back to Brushy.

By 1903, when Daddy was born, the country around Brushy Creek was mostly farmland and southern in culture. But Daddy was a Barker and their roots were deep and old, southern and western mixed. Horses and cattle were still very much part of the family. Daddy grew up farming and ranching. He had good teachers. And he had that all-too-rare characteristic of humans: He knew who he was and where he lived. His roots were so well anchored in that blackland prairie that he was unaware of them, but he knew the stories that went with them, the stories that held the family to that place as surely as the grass roots had once held the prairie together.

Daddy had gone to Texas A&M and taken a degree in animal husbandry. He had learned the latest techniques, had mastered the most up-to-date theories of managing land and livestock. And he had shown his gift with horses. He was offered two jobs when he graduated, one as the manager of a large ranch in West Texas, the other in the horse program at the King Ranch. When I was nearing the end of my college years, I asked Daddy why he hadn't taken either of those jobs, especially the one on the King Ranch, a job that would have led to his helping to develop the modern quarter horse breed and to work with such Thoroughbreds as Assault, who won the Kentucky Derby in about '48 or '49. He told me he'd rather work for himself, make his own decisions on a small, struggling place, than to be working for someone else on the biggest ranch in the world. I remember that as good advice, even today.

While most of that end of the country in Daddy's lifetime was covered with cotton and grain, he could look over it and see, in his mind's eye, the tall grass prairie, wave after wave, to the horizon. Daddy was a farmer and a rancher, a resident of the Deep South and the West, and a bridge between the horse-and-buggy days and modern times; and Daddy was both storyteller and teacher. Daddy's eyes are dimmed with age now, but it has only been the last five years that I have thought of him as old. Maybe it was the fact that he remained active into his eighties. Perhaps it was because I can't remember him as a young man; he was considered old, as a father, when I was born. Daddy wasn't big (he played college football at about 135 pounds) except for his hands. Daddy was maybe fifty when I first noticed how big his hands were. A lifetime of milking and handling teams has that effect. Today his hair still has as much pepper as salt, back then it was black. And black eyebrows show off Irish blue eyes to good effect. You'd have thought Daddy was dark complected until he came inside, then you saw his fair forehead, protected by a hat whenever he was outside. He always took his hat off when he was inside, but I never remember seeing him bareheaded outside. After I was grown, I thought of how Daddy was so relaxed around the house, so I asked him how he managed to never bring any of his problems home with him.

"I carry my problems in my hat," he said. "That way when I take my hat off, I leave my problems with it."

It's quite an idea. The fascinating thing is that it works, as did his other admonition about his work philosophy: "You can't farm or ranch without a sense of humor. Without a sense of humor, you can't make it in a business where you buy everything retail, sell everything wholesale, and let the other fellow set the prices."

I was about ten, Daddy about fifty-four, the first time one of Daddy's stories hit me with the full weight of place behind it. I'd been carrying on about something, maybe how wild the country was in a Western I'd seen at the Saturday matinee. Anyway, my conversation was running along the lines of things being too civilized. Daddy let me run my string out as long as I wanted. Then, just as we were coming to Cottonwood Creek, he said, "Right down there, Grandpa Barker killed a bear. After he shot her, two cubs came out of the brush. It was the spring of the year and the cubs were tiny, so he caught them. He said it was quite a little chase, around and around, until he got them into a to'e sack and tied the neck off with a piece of whang leather. They lay

17

still for a little while, but then, as bear cubs are wont to do, they got to tussling around in the bag, either trying to get out or wrestling with each other. Grandpa was busy cleaning the bear and quartering her so he could pack the meat and hide home. He didn't really pay any attention to the cubs. When he had finished, he looked back around for the cubs and didn't see the sack. He remembered how they'd been tussling around and figured they'd gotten out. After he'd looked around for the empty sack for a few minutes, he gave up and went down to the creek to wash his hands and knife. There, out in the water, was the sack. The cubs, wrestling around, had rolled off the bank and out into the creek and drowned. He hadn't meant for that to happen, of course, but once it had he speculated that it may well have been for the best. The cubs would have wreaked havoc on the place if he'd taken them home, and he'd have deserved it for trying to make pets out of wild animals."

At that moment you might say history jumped out and slapped me in the face. I realized that Daddy had been living on that same piece of ground for over half a century and that Grandpa Barker, one of the first whites who'd moved out onto the prairie around there, had camped there for the first time only sixty or so years before Daddy was born. I looked over the plowed fields, still late-winter bare but soon to be covered with cotton, corn, and maize, and I saw grass, the long rolling waves of prairie grasses that had been there when Grandpa Barker had killed the bear. I touched the land—ancient deep black soil—and realized that Daddy was as deeply rooted there as the tall grasses, or the pecan trees along the creeks. I too, through the stories Daddy told, was an inheritor of the prairie of bears and wild horses as much as the cotton fields I could see with my everyday eyes.

Daddy saw that way. In a half century he had seen it change from a horse-drawn world to a mechanized one; he had seen the pasturelands shrink as tractors made more land available to the plow. Beyond his personal memories there were his contacts with the past. He had as a child spent much time with Grandpa Barker and Granddaddy Garry. He had listened to stories of the area as wilderness, of the development of the cattle business, and of early attempts at subsistence farming. Daddy's uncles were full of stories of the changes that happened once plows were developed to break the heavy black soil and deep sod and the railroad brought many farmers and a way to ship the cotton that flourished in the deep, black prairie soil.

At age twelve Daddy had begun to work for Uncle Emzy during the summers. Uncle Emzy was as good a horseman as there was around there and he paid Daddy with an education second to none. Daddy was riding Coly then, as good a horse as you could ask for (good enough that I recognized him the first time I saw a picture of him—Daddy talked that fondly of him and described him that well). Uncle Emzy spent several summers teaching Daddy what you could ask of a good horse and how to get it to respond. He taught by example, by coaching, and by hard lessons. Once, at the end of a long day, he caught Daddy slouching with all his weight on one foot. Uncle Emzy reached down and tapped Coly on the hock, causing him to kick and very nearly spilling Daddy. When Daddy complained he was tired, Uncle Emzy told him that Coly was too, but that if you rode a horse like you were proud to be on him he'd respond by being proud to carry you, even if you were both tired. Daddy never slouched after that. When Daddy went to Texas A&M in 1921, he was amazed to discover that most of the students who were in the cavalry (A&M was still a military school then) weren't horsemen. But the teachers weren't amazed. They were more surprised to find a horseman. Mr. Garrigan, in particular, became one of Daddy's mentors. Mr. Garrigan was in charge of the stables, was a trainer and a racer of trotting and pacing horses, and was, in those days, considered one of the best horsemen in the country. He and Daddy became fast friends and he spent much more time working with Daddy than with other students. I always regretted that Mr. Garrigan died before my time, because Mother said that, for as long as he was there, trips to A&M for football games involved as much time at the stables as anywhere else. Daddy finished A&M a horseman, educated in the cavalry school, dressage, jumping and harness work, as well as the cowboy way that Uncle Emzy had started him in.

I had watched Daddy ride all my life. He was so natural, so joined to the horse, that I didn't realize how many years had gone into making such a horseman; I only knew he was a horseman. He was a great teacher, and in riding, as in life, he taught partly by example. I spent the first two years of my riding career, from ages three to five, in a "pony ring" with Daddy standing in the center, coaching. For a year or so after that I could ride only with him, my brother Buz, or my sister Grace Mary. By then I had the image of what a horseman should look like fixed in my head and I worked to achieve that vision. When I was about twelve, Daddy let me start using his spurs. I was so proud of those spurs I wouldn't have thought of getting on a horse without them. It was many years before I realized that Daddy had given me the long-shanked spurs for the same reason Uncle Emzy had given them to him when he was twelve. With those long shanks, you couldn't get sloppy and let your toes turn out. If you did, the shanks caused the spurs to jab the horse and keep it buzzed up. So without having to do any more coaching on the subject, Daddy made sure that I learned to carry my feet properly. Today, thirty-odd years later, I still have the spurs—and I still don't let my toes turn out.

I did, of course, reach a level, as I think most boys do, of thinking I'd learned everything there was to know. I got to thinking that I truly was the inheritor of the grasslands and the horsemen who had preceded the plow. By the time I entered junior high—and puberty—I was getting pretty cocky about my abilities. I'd graduated from falling heir to old horses to buying younger ones. I'd bought Miss Kitty, an eight-year-old dun mare, from Clyde Arnold, a good cowboy and horseman from Briggs. She was my "using" horse. And Larry Zimmerhanzel had sold me a beautiful little bay filly that I was training myself. At least in my mind I was training the filly myself; I may have been over-looking the fact that Daddy and Manuel were telling me everything I needed to know to do the training. I guess Daddy finally had enough of my new, greatly expanded hat size, because one day, as we were crossing Mustang Creek on our way into town, Daddy pointed up the creek and said,

"Grandpa Barker and Calvin" (his brother) "were headed home one time when Calvin's horse pulled up lame. There was a ford down there then—it was still there when I was a kid—and the brush was too thick even to think about crossing except at the fords. There was a band of mustangs feeding in that big flat south of the creek, so Calvin staked out the ford and Grandpa Barker rode up to the next one, a mile or so up the creek. When he came back down, he got behind the mustangs and stampeded them across the ford. Calvin roped the one he wanted when it went by and hung on until Grandpa Barker came up and got another rope on it. Then he snubbed it up short while Calvin got his saddle on it and they went on home."

I tried to imagine what it took to catch a wild horse and ride it home. Aside from any question of getting bucked off, just trying to keep it pointed in the right direction seemed far more trouble than walking the eight miles home, even if you had to carry your saddle. So I asked the obvious question: "Why didn't Calvin just walk home?"

"Calvin wasn't much of a pedestrian," Daddy replied.

It was several years before I again referred to myself as a horseman. Even today I am hesitant to use the term without qualifiers. Daddy was as good a teacher as he was a horseman. His teaching was generally something as simple as a story. He seldom told me things directly. Instead, he'd ask me if he'd ever told me about the time that ... and there would follow a story that illustrated whatever he wanted me to know. He knew that I remembered stories. Whenever I was back in the context of the story, I'd recall it and the lesson would be there to affect my behavior. The stories covered all aspects of horses (and everything else for that matter), from the most serious matters to the simple business of how to tell whether a horse was good-looking.

Uncle Rufe, while still a young man, had been blinded during a minor misunderstanding about who belonged to some money. The other man had bird shot rather than buckshot in his shotgun, so Uncle Rufe came out of the debate alive but blind. When Daddy was a big kid, he'd take Uncle Rufe downtown to join the other old men who spent the afternoons chewing tobacco, whittling, and telling stories to one another.

"I was sitting with him one day," Daddy said, "listening to them telling lies to one another. There was a politeness about it, like the story of the man watching a poker game.

He noticed that one of the men was cheating and whispered his observation to one of the other players. The other player responded, 'Well, of course he is; it's his deal, isn't it?' Anyway, while we were sitting there, a stranger rode by on a sure-'nough good horse. Two or three of the men commented on the horse the man was riding. Then Uncle Rufe piped up and said, 'Yeah, and he's fat and slicked off good too.' 'How could you tell?' everyone asked in amazement. 'By the sound of his hooves,' Uncle Rufe replied.

"When we were walking home, I asked Uncle Rufe how he could tell by the sound of the horse's hooves that it was fat and sleek. 'I couldn't,' he replied. 'But stop and think a minute. Have you ever seen a horse that people would brag on that wasn't fat and sleek?' "

I don't suppose I've heard anyone brag on a good horse since then and not thought of Uncle Rufe. Stories carry information in an easily remembered form—if they're told in a context that sets the stage for the telling and provides a trigger for the memory the next time you need it. Daddy was a master of placing stories in context.

We were standing on the north rim of the Grand Canyon (actually, we were standing back from the rim a bit: Daddy was a plainsman and not a great fan of heights) when a dude asked Daddy if we were from Texas. I think most dudes assume you're from Texas if you wear a Stetson hat. Daddy got to visiting with him and, after he'd established that Daddy raised a few cows when there was enough rain to grow grass, he asked how much land we had. Now, that's a question about like asking a dude how much money he has in the bank and Daddy saw my eyebrows go up as we waited for his reply. It was, as I should have expected from Daddy, polite but vague. After the dude had left, Daddy turned to me and said,

"I took Uncle Emzy to visit Uncle Frate one time, right

after Uncle Frate had bought a new pasture that joined his place at Manchaca. We got over there in the late afternoon, but it was still hot enough to hunt shade so I parked the Model T under a live oak down by his barn. Uncle Frate came in about the same time. After he'd tended to his horse and put his saddle away, he invited us up to the house for some ice tea and a visit.

"Once we were settled on the gallery and had established that everyone's family was well, Uncle Emzy asked Uncle Frate if he'd bought a new pasture.

" 'Yeah.' (Remember that yeah, where I come from, is a word of two or three syllables with no clear-cut ending.)

" 'How big?'

" 'Big enough.'

" 'How are the fences?'

" 'Need a little work in places.'

" 'Water?'

" 'Has some.'

" 'What'll it carry?'

" 'Everything I got to put on it.'

"Uncle Emzy gave up then and they talked of other things, mostly the old days, before the country was fenced. And I reflected on the fact that you don't have to be rude even if the question you're asked is. Uncle Emzy thought a brother could ask such a question; that fellow from back East just didn't know any better."

You know, it works; I used the idea myself just last fall when Joe Medicine Crow and I were in San Francisco. I was sitting in the hotel lobby when a fellow sat down next to me and we fell to visiting. Once he'd established that I was living on a ranch in Wyoming, he asked how big it was. "Well," I told him, "from high ground everything I can see belongs to the Thrones, one of their neighbors, or the government." I guess that satisfied him; he didn't ask any further.

I'll admit that it's really hard to ask appropriate questions about a culture you know nothing about. For that reason we tend to be forgiving of people's misunderstandings, provided they're polite. One problem of being part of a culture that changes slowly is that, taken as a whole, this has always been a country—a people—engaged in the process of becoming something. We've always been going somewhere. The U.S. has always been a place of doers, of movers and shakers. Fortunately, we've always had some folks who were willing to settle down and just *be*. I think, up until recently, most of the men who fell into that category were whittlers. Whittling—as opposed to carving, which is concerned with making something—is probably the only truly American form of meditation. If whittling has any purpose other than meditation, it is to clear the mind enough to dip into the passing stream of oral tradition for stories. Mostly, though, it is simply a way of being. I'm a whittler, descended from a long line of whittlers, no one of whom has ever had ulcers or other nervous complaints. As is the case with any art form, there are master whittlers. The best I've ever encountered, in life or fiction, was Uncle Bob.

Uncle Bob had grown up in slower times in the last century. He had learned his pacing from horses and mules, and though he'd made some concessions to the twentieth century he continued to pace himself by natural rhythms. And he continued to whittle. Uncle Bob died before my time, but Daddy told me enough about him for me to know him well. He owned a meat market and a house in Austin as well as land outside of town. He lived into the hard times of the

Depression, but by then he'd turned much of the operation of the ranch and the meat market over to his children. Still, he liked to check on things himself.

"One afternoon," Daddy told me, "Uncle Bob had been checking on things at the meat market. Of course everything was running smoothly, so he adjourned to the sidewalk in front of the store. The curb there was high enough for comfortable sitting, so he sat down and started to whittle. It was a hot day but, as the afternoon progressed, the shadow of the building fell over him, so Uncle Bob took off his hat and set it down next to him." (A little aside here for those of you who go around bareheaded all the time: Always set your hat down bottom side up, to prevent your luck from running out of it.) "Uncle Bob continued to whittle until they closed the meat market and one of the boys came out to take him home. By then he had a pretty good sized pile of shavings around his feet and not much left of the piece of cedar he'd started with. He had thought his thoughts all afternoon, without giving much attention to anything going on around him. So he was quite surprised at the cascade of coins that spilled from his hat when he put it on. Cities were full of beggars during the Depression, and people walking past the white-haired old gentleman had naturally mistaken his upturned hat for a solicitation. Uncle Bob said he'd never thought of whittling as an occupation before, but that from then on he always took his hat off when he whittled in public."

"What did Uncle Bob do with the shavings when he was finished?" I asked Daddy. (I was going through a practical phase at that time.)

"Well," he replied, "if he was at home he kept them to use for starting fires. They still had a woodburning stove in the kitchen and either a fireplace or a stove in every room.

But in front of the meat market, or anywhere else in town, he'd just fish a match out of his pocket and burn the pile right there. I don't guess you could do that anymore, but I saw him sitting on the curb down on Congress Avenue one time, visiting with someone, could have been Mr. Petmakey. They were both whittling, of course. I was across the street and maybe a block or so down, just coming out of a store, when I saw a city cop walking up to them. I figured he'd make them move, since no one could park where they were sitting, but instead he sat down with them and started visiting. I crossed the street and started toward them. They must have been sitting there a good while, because the pile in front of Uncle Bob was knee-high and two or three feet across. As I approached, the three of them stood up, Uncle Bob dropped a lit match into the pile of shavings, and they all walked away, the cop and Mr. Petmakey one way and Uncle Bob over to me, proposing that a cup of coffee would be nice about then. We walked off to the Driskill coffee shop, leaving a bonfire burning behind us."

Fortunately, that relatively short practical phase in my life was balanced with the beginning of a phase that asked what I see now as more important questions. One day I was sitting outside the smokehouse, trying to whittle on a hackberry limb, when it dawned on me that good whittlers probably had preferred woods—and hackberry wasn't one of them. So I asked Daddy about it.

"Uncle Bob and Aunt Monty had a house in town as well as out at the ranch," Daddy started in. "Aunt Monty told me that one time—this would have been when they were older and more or less retired—she looked out the kitchen window and saw a fellow pull into the driveway with a Model T truck loaded with cedar fence posts. As she told me: 'It was along in the middle of the morning and I was baking and didn't really need any interruptions, but I stopped and wiped my hands and went out to tell that old cedar-whacker that we didn't need any fence posts. By the time I got outside he was piling posts next to the buggy house.

" 'Here,' I told him. 'What are you doing?'

" 'Mr. Bob bought these from me, told me to deliver them.'

" 'Well, take them out to the place. We don't have any fences here in town.'

" 'Oh, no, ma'am,' the cedar-whacker said. 'Mr. Bob said to bring them here. These posts aren't for fence fixing, they're for whittling.'

"Uncle Bob was as serious a whittler as I ever knew," Daddy concluded, "and he wouldn't use anything but good cedar. He said that not only did it feel the best to work with but it smelled good too."

I started using cedar then and, though I've tried other woods since, I'm still convinced that Uncle Bob was right. There's usually at least one or two sticks in the back of the pickup, just in case I have the time and the opportunity.

At about that same time I had started to carry a good pocketknife, had discovered hard Arkansas stones, and, with a little coaching from Daddy, had learned to keep an edge on my knife. One day Daddy saw me pulling my knife toward me as I worked around a little knot on the piece of cedar I was whittling on.

"Back before radio and movies," he told me with no other preamble, "when there were still tent shows, an advance man showed up in Taylor and posted handbills all over town announcing the arrival of a show the next day. Small shows like that usually didn't draw much of a crowd, but the handbills for that one got everyone's attention; they said,

'Something every man should know! Absolutely no women or children allowed!'

"The next day, my daddy told me, when the time for the show arrived, every male in Taylor over the age of about twelve or fourteen who could raise a nickel was waiting outside the tent. There were enough folks working for the outfit to sell tickets and a big enough fellow taking tickets that no one sneaked in. There weren't any seats in the tent, so they crammed everyone inside at once. Then, with necks craned to see better, everyone waited in expectant silence as the curtain rose and revealed an old man sitting on the stage, whittling. When he was sure he had the crowd's full and undivided attention, he looked out over the house and said, 'Always whittle away from you.' The curtain went down and the show was over. Fortunately, someone started laughing and the male population of Taylor, rather than getting mad and tearing the tent apart, decided to join in the joke."

By the time I came along, tent shows were pretty much a thing of the past. A few circuses still survived, playing under the big top, but radio, movies, and TV had killed the tent shows. I mourned their demise because I'd heard so many stories about them, but I was a reasonably normal kid. I went to school, played Little League baseball, listened to the radio, and watched TV—but not on school nights—after we got one. And I went to the movies, or the picture show, as we said then. Most Saturdays we'd listen to the Chicago market report while we ate a dinner of brown beans and ham hock, fried corn bread and coleslaw; then Daddy took Grace Mary, Buz, and me into town for the matinee at the picture show—a cartoon or two, the newsreel, some commercials, tags for coming attractions, a serial, and, if we were lucky, a double feature, at least one of which was a B Western. We saw everyone from Gene and Roy to Rex Allen, Tim Holt, Johnny MacBrown, to Whip Wilson and Lash Larue. We were regular listeners to radio Westerns: "Gene Autry," "The Lone Ranger," and "Gunsmoke." We acquired our first TV in the late fifties, during the heyday of Westerns like "Have Gun Will Travel," "Gunsmoke," "Maverick," "Wagon Train," and "Bonanza." Like any kid growing up in America during those years, I had a good grounding in the West of Hollywood—the West of myth. But unlike most kids, I had something to measure the myth against: Uncle Dud. He was the youngest of Daddy's uncles and one of the last of the old-time western lawmen. He'd joined the Texas Rangers in the 1890s, when they were still organized into the frontier battalions. He'd quit the Rangers to marry and had ranched for several years before becoming sheriff of Pecos County, Texas. He was sheriff for twenty-odd turbulent years. And he had told Daddy, his favorite nephew, most all his stories. I was fascinated with the idea that there were people like Matt Dillon and Paladin in my family, so I was constantly prodding him for tales about Uncle Dud. The stories started with the incidents around a big feud at San Saba just a year or so after Uncle Dud joined the Rangers. This is how Daddy told the story:

"That was the tail end of the days of the vigilante committees. Most of them started with the best of intentions—to make their communities a better place to live—but there was no way to control them, since no one would reveal who belonged. All too often these committees would wind up being used to cover up all manner of crimes. When that happened in San Saba, another group formed to fight the first one and a sure-'nough feud developed. There was a judge and a district attorney willing to prosecute the guilty parties, but people were afraid to testify because no one was sure who might be listening and what the vigilante committee would do if word got back to its members. So the judge wrote to the governor and the call went out for the Rangers. Uncle Dud was in the Ranger company sent there to assure that a grand jury could meet and that people could feel safe to testify. The Rangers were there over a year.

"The Rangers camped on the river a few miles out of town so there could be no question of their taking sides in the feud by staying with someone who might be a principle: This measure also kept down the costs to the state. Making sure that the camp was safe and that no one would come by to look through their papers was a problem for the Rangers. In the first few weeks one of the Rangers had to stay in camp at all times. Then John L. Sullivan, the oldest of the Rangers and no kin to the prizefighter of the same name, left for a few days and returned with a huge, fierce-looking bulldog. In reality the dog was nothing more than an overgrown puppy who wanted to play with everyone. Sullivan put a huge chain on his collar, though, and tied him to a tree. When people saw the dog straining to get at them, Sullivan told them it was a killer guard dog. He reassured them that it was safe when the Rangers were around because they kept him tied up then, but he warned them not to come around when no one was there because the dog was loose then. In a few days word had gotten around and no one would dare to venture near the camp. The Rangers' papers were as well protected as they would have been in a safe.

"Feelings were running high all over that end of the world, though, and there were enough people involved in the feud that the Rangers were constantly on their guard. The principals were afraid of the grand jury, once the Rangers arrived, because then people were willing to testify. Over a period of several months the situation got tense enough that anything could have set it off. Uncle Dud was in his early twenties and looked younger. Looking so young may have contributed to his being involved when things came to a head. But it was tamales that set off the chain of events.

"Uncle Dud was in town one day," Daddy told me, "when he encountered three men who the Rangers were sure, but couldn't yet prove, were principals in the feud. One of them had been bragging for weeks about how he wasn't afraid of the Rangers. On that day, when Uncle Dud saw him trying to bully a tamale vendor, his bragging was backed up with whiskey." (Tamale vendors were a staple of that part of the world up into the 1950s. Working from pushcarts, they walked the streets hawking their wares, generally with the cry "Hot! Hot tamales!" The cry was so distinctive that Taylor's last tamale vendor went by the name Hot.) "The braggart and his friends had stopped on their way from one saloon to the next to eat some tamales. When they had finished, the other two paid for their tamales but the braggart refused to. He may have done it to anyone, but the fact that the vendor was black may have increased the braggart's willingness to bully him. Uncle Dud saw what was going on and stepped in. He forced the man to pay and told his friends to get him home and sober him up. Uncle Dud didn't think anything of it at the time. About an hour later, as Uncle Dud walked down one of the streets facing the courthouse, the braggart came around the corner fifty feet in front of him and leveled a Winchester at him. Before the man could fire, Uncle Dud drew his pistol and shot him dead center. He said the man doubled over at the impact but pulled himself erect and tried to level the rifle again. Uncle Dud shot him again, killing him. Uncle Dud got scared then, because he was alone, and his rifle was across the street on his horse. He started toward his horse, ejecting the empty cartridges as he walked. About the middle of the street he pulled a fresh box of bullets from his pocket and dropped it. He figured everyone would think he was scared and some friend of the man he'd just killed might see that as an excuse to try to shoot him. So he took out his handkerchief and cleaned off every bullet; then he loaded his pistol and put the rest of the dusted bullets back into the box. By the time he'd finished a couple more Rangers had arrived, and it was clear that the dead man's friends hadn't accompanied him to the square.

"That incident, on top of the work the Rangers had been doing, seemed to take the wind out of the vigilantes' sails. Within a short time, the grand jury returned a pretty good crowd of true bills and the feud was over."

That was Uncle Dud's first shooting incident. Daddy told me that story and many others while I was a kid. For the last several years I've been documenting those incidents. That was the only one while he was a Ranger; most of the rest happened during his years as sheriff of Pecos County. Most are available in courthouse records and old newspapers. Many of the accounts Uncle Dud had in his personal files. But one of the stories seems to have traveled only by word of mouth. It happened long after Uncle Dud had retired and moved to Alpine. I remember it well since it was one of Daddy's favorites.

"The fellow who told me the story," Daddy said, "was from around Taylor; he was just visiting out in Alpine when it happened. He and the family he was visiting were awakened one night by the sound of a fight next door. This is the story he told me.

" 'We got out of bed to see what was going on. It turned

out not to be a fight but a man beating his wife. He'd hit their boy, a kid in his teens, two or three times, but the kid had gotten out of the house. The wife wasn't so lucky. The kid ran onto our porch and started pounding on the front door, begging us to let him in and to call the police. We got him in and my friend called the cops while his wife tended to the shiner the kid had. I looked out and saw a crowd gathering, not big, but a half dozen were there already and I could see lights in houses up and down the street and more people coming out onto their porches. No one was going up to the house where the beating was going on; folks were just standing around out by the curb like they didn't want to get too close. From the sounds coming out of the house I didn't blame them. My friend came out onto the porch where I was standing and told me that all the sheriff's people were out on calls but that he'd phoned Dud Barker.

" 'Coming from Taylor, I knew that name. I'd heard Dud Barker stories—stories of blood and thunder, of six-shooters and quick draws, the Texas Rangers back in the old days. I waited, expecting Randolph Scott or John Wayne to ride up on a pacing stallion. Instead, I saw a Chrysler pull up, and an old, gray-haired man in a three-piece suit climbed out. He had on a Stetson hat and cowboy boots but, other than that, he looked more like a banker than a lawman. He wasn't exactly John Wayne's size either. He was maybe five foot six or seven inches tall and I doubt he weighed over 135 pounds. But the crowd on the curb—there were fifteen or twenty folks standing around out there by then—opened a path and let him through. He walked up on the front porch of that house just as calm as you please and knocked on the door. Nothing happened, so he knocked again, louder.

" 'Maybe ten seconds after that second knock the man came boiling out the door. I mean, he like to have ripped the screen door off its hinges. And he was as big as John Wayne. He must have been six foot six and was powerfully built. He didn't have on a shirt, just an undershirt, and you could see, in the glow from the streetlight there on the corner, how heavily muscled up he was. He looked twice the size of your uncle. He stood there towering over Mr. Barker and glaring down at him. His fists were hanging by his side; they looked like he was holding a couple of hams. Mr. Barker just stood there, as relaxed as though he'd been invited there for supper. Finally, the man said, 'Damn you, Dud, I might just break you in half. And what can you do about it?'

" 'Well, your uncle just looked at him and smiled. Now remember, I was standing on the porch of the house next door, at right angles to them, and I was close enough to see really clearly. And believe you me, I was watching and listening really hard. Well, your uncle just looked at him, smiled, and said, 'Well, I guess I could kill you.' I never saw your uncle move, but when he said that he had a .45 tucked into that fellow's mid-section. It was that fast, no flurry, no nothing. The gun was just there. That mass of muscle I'd been so impressed with a few minutes before just seemed to deflate. Really, it was like all the air had been let out of him. He must have felt that pistol pressed in under his ribs, but he didn't look at it. He was looking into that old man's eyes. I couldn't see his eyes, but I could tell what that fellow was seeing in them. The fight was out of him and he was sobering up rapidly. Mr. Barker took that fellow out to the streetlight in front of his house, had him reach around the pole, and he handcuffed him there. Then he told some of the women who were standing there to go in and help the man's wife.

" 'I don't know what happened after that. The kid went

back to help his mother and we went back to bed. Somebody said your uncle dropped the handcuff key off at the sheriff's office. Someone else said he just went home and came back the next morning and turned the guy loose. Whatever he did, my friends told me that the man hasn't had a drink since then.' "

Even though Uncle Dud was shot at a number of times, he was never hit. The whole time he was sheriff the closest he ever came to being killed was by a pan of biscuits.

"It was back around 1908 or '10," Daddy said, "when a cowboy rode up to the sheriff's office at Fort Stockton and told Uncle Dud that he'd found a dead man at a campsite about fifteen miles out of town. He said he hadn't touched anything as he figured Uncle Dud would want to investigate. By the time Uncle Dud finished what he had to do in town, rounded up the coroner, and got a horse harnessed to his buckboard, it was getting late. By the time they got out to the body there wasn't much daylight left. After looking at the signs, the coroner said it looked like the man apparently had had a heart attack or some sort of seizure while he was eating his supper. Uncle Dud noticed from the tracks that the man had hobbled his horses before he'd turned them loose, so he went looking for them while the coroner cleaned up the camp. When he got back with the horses, he found that the coroner had started fixing supper, making do with what he'd found in the camp—a kitchen outfit, some canned goods, flour and baking powder. Neither of them had a chance to eat before leaving town, so they were hungry. Uncle Dud watered the horses, hitched them to the off side of the man's wagon, and started going through his papers, trying to figure out who he had been, while the coroner fixed supper. He'd made up a batch of biscuits and had them cooking in the man's Dutch oven when Uncle Dud looked up and saw a rider coming toward them in the twilight. Uncle Dud said he recognized the man from the way he sat his horse: It was a rancher who lived another twenty or so miles on to the east. They figured the man would be hungry by the time he got to the camp, so they waited supper on him. When he stopped out a ways and helloed the camp, as range etiquette required, Uncle Dud called him by name, told him who he was, and invited him to supper. By the time he'd tended to his horse and joined us the coroner had stirred up a slumgullion and the coffee was ready. He was scraping the coals from the lid of the Dutch oven full of biscuits when the rancher told Uncle Dud how happy he was to find him because he was tracking a man in a wagon who had stopped by his ranch while nobody was home. 'What did he steal?' Uncle Dud asked. But the rancher said nothing was stolen, the man had only taken some food." (Range etiquette again. That was acceptable behavior in such big country. Where towns were few and far between, it was accepted that you fed people who stopped by, even if you weren't there. Passing a ranch house when no one was home just made the stop self-service. People were expected to either bring food on a return trip or simply extend the courtesy to some other wayfarer later.) "The problem was, the rancher explained, the baking powder can the man had taken was filled with strychnine he used for poisoning coyotes.

"Uncle Dud said the coroner stopped scraping ashes off the Dutch oven and started panting. He said that though he'd had a long hard day, hadn't eaten since an early breakfast, and had been starving a few seconds earlier, he completely lost his appetite. While the coroner was burning up the biscuits, Uncle Dud gave the rancher a thorough tongue-lashing about keeping poison in a food container.

"The rancher caught his horse and headed home before Uncle Dud could think of some excuse to arrest him for stupidity; Uncle Dud and the coroner decided to head back to town since they had not only lost their appetites but found that they weren't at all sleepy either. He said he drove the man's wagon and the coroner drove the buckboard, and even though they were side by side, neither one said a word all the way back to town.

"Uncle Dud said when he got in late that night, he went into his kids' rooms and just looked at them and thought how lucky he was to see them. The next morning he put the strychnine in a can marked poison, burned the baking powder can, and shot a hole in the bottom of the Dutch oven. He never told me how long it was before he could eat biscuits again."

I still go out to Fort Stockton and Alpine to collect stories about Uncle Dud; there are plenty of folks who remember him. When I listen to them talk, it's easy to visualize that country ninety or a hundred years ago. It hasn't changed all that much. There are places where I collect stories where it's harder to see through time. There are places—too many of them—that have been so changed that serious effort is needed. And it gets harder ever year. Daddy never tired of helping Grace Mary, Buz, and me to see our home: to see it through time. When Margaret Grace (one of Buz's daughters) was about five, I realized Daddy was still at it.

Buz still lives on the home place, but Grace Mary and I are a long way from Texas. When both of us get there at the same time, it's a cause for celebration. It was on such an occasion when we were driving the thirty-five miles to Austin to have Sunday brunch at Green Pastures, always a special treat for all of us. Green Pastures is old, beautiful, and, as Margaret Grace quickly pointed out, had the best cheese biscuits south of Grammy's house. As we drove down Congress Avenue, Daddy asked Margaret Grace if she remembered the streetcars that used to run on Congress Avenue. She laughed at him, already knowing at age five that her Paw Paw sometimes asked questions for effect rather than answers.

"When I was a boy," Daddy told her, "about thirteen or fourteen years old, I came over here with Uncle Emzy to help drive a herd of mules back to Brushy. Uncle Frate had wintered them and we needed to get them back because Uncle Emzy had plenty of cotton farmers lined up to sell them to. Austin wasn't nearly as big as it is now. Green Pastures, where we're going this morning, was out about the edge of town. Uncle Frate's place at Manchaca was several miles south of Austin. We rode the train from Taylor over here and Uncle Frate had someone meet us and take us out to his place. We had supper, a good visit, and went to bed early.

"We ate breakfast in the dark and had the mules on the road long before daylight. Uncle Emzy was leading and they were following pretty well. Uncle Frate's son, Robert, and I were on one side of them, a hired hand on the other, and Uncle Frate was behind them keeping them moving. Our plan was to take them right up Congress Avenue and out Manor Road. We figured to have the mules through downtown before there was any traffic to worry about. When we came down South Congress, we had the mules pretty well crowded together and were making good time; hadn't seen any cars and very few people. There was a different bridge over the Colorado on Congress Avenue back then, but it was just as long as the one here today. And it had tracks for the streetcars. We were just short of halfway over it when a streetcar pulled onto the north end of the bridge and started across. Thirty-some-odd head of mules froze when they saw the streetcar coming at them. They'd never seen anything like that before in their lives and they weren't sure if it was coming to eat them or what. If the streetcar operator had known anything about mules, he'd have stopped and we could probably have gotten the mules past it in a few minutes. But I don't think he knew any more about mules than they knew about streetcars; he kept coming. Then, when the mules were quivering with fear at the approaching streetcar, he rang its bell. Mules exploded all over that bridge. Several of them headed for the edge of the bridge, but the long drop to the river was a bit too much for them. They wheeled and ran. We were behind them by then and kept them from heading back south. When the first one made it past the streetcar, more or less by accident, the rest saw it could be done and followed. When they cleared the north end of the bridge, they turned east down First Street and scattered all over that part of Austin."

"How ever did you find them, Paw Paw?" Margaret Grace, the world's only five-year-old who would say how ever, asked.

"Well," Daddy continued, "it wasn't that hard to find the mules. All that part of Austin was houses back then. It was early morning, in the spring of the year, warm enough for everyone to be sleeping with their windows open, and of course no one had screens on their windows back then. Once the mules had gotten over their panic from the streetcar, their natural curiosity took over. When they saw curtains waving in the breeze, they'd go over to investigate. When people woke up to see a mule sticking its head through their bedroom window, they screamed loud enough for us to locate most of the mules. It only took an hour or so to gather them all again. We had to deal with some traffic when we got back to Congress Avenue, but by then the mules were either getting used to town or were too tired to care; we didn't have any more trouble. Once we got through Austin, we made good time and had the mules in Uncle Emzy's pens by suppertime. Not counting all the running around catching the mules, we covered a bit over forty miles that day. Now, little girl, if we'd ridden over here horseback, by the time we got to Green Pastures, you'd be able to eat all the cheese biscuits in the world."

"Oh, Paw Paw," Margaret Grace laughed, "I can do that when we ride over here in a car."

I listened to Daddy and thought of the impossibility of driving mules through Austin today. Aside from the fact that there is no time of the day or night when there is not more automobile traffic than Daddy would have seen at the height of a business day back then, I'm sure the police department would take a dim view of even suggesting such an activity. The world has changed. Since I've never been able to see too far back in cities, I allowed my mind to drift back to the end of Daddy's story, thinking about how considerably things had changed at home in my lifetime let alone in Daddy's. Changes are often marked by the comings and goings of people. I suppose that and the story of horses and mules led me to think about Manuel. Manuel Valdez came to work for Daddy when I was about seven years old. His brother-in-law, Pedro Ortegon, had worked for Daddy for several years. When I was introduced to the writings of Nobel laureate Juan Ramon Jimenez years later, I always imagined that he looked like Pedro: tall, to a five-year-old, spare, and incredibly dignified, with a goatee and mustache. Manuel came to work on Pedro's recommendation and he stayed. He was as lean as Pedro but very small. He was the size of a jockey, maybe 110 pounds at the most. His white hair was shoulder length, and his full, wonderfully grizzled beard rested on his chest. His eyes were as deep and pure and peaceful as any I have ever encountered. Manuel was one of the finest horsemen I ever hope to meet. He was also the only person I've known who could actually talk with animals. Dogs who were unruly around others were well behaved around Manuel, even though he didn't use any of the standard disciplinary techniques; he just talked to them. They actually seemed to be embarrassed to misbehave in his presence.

Old fighting cows with young calves, cows that would attack anyone or anything approaching them and their calves, allowed him to walk beside them and scratch their backs. Manuel spoke most animal languages at least as well as he spoke English and perhaps as well as Spanish. The first horse I trained—well, the first horse I thought I trained; actually, Daddy and Manuel were training both of us—was a beautiful little bay filly I named Poca Bonita. With Daddy and Manuel coaching me, I'd worked her slowly, from gentling and halterbreaking her to working her with long lines. But Daddy didn't figure I was ready, at age twelve, to be the first one to ride her. On the appointed day Daddy rode Miss Kitty, my good using horse, and Manuel rode the filly. Poca had been led enough and Manuel was light enough that there wasn't any problem until Daddy let go of the lead rope. When she realized that she wasn't being led and that someone was on her back, she became tentative in her movements. When Manuel asked her to turn, Poca started to, then threw her head up and followed it with her body. As she reared, Manuel moved with a fluidity that, unobserved, would not be believed. He was suddenly standing with his feet in the seat of the saddle and pulling back on the reins. Poca staggered backward, Manuel keeping her just past her balance point until she couldn't back up fast enough and came over backwards, not hard, and with enough control to land on her side. Before she could move, Manuel was lying over Poca's neck, holding her head so she couldn't get up. Daddy motioned me back as I started forward to try to help. But I was close enough to hear as Manuel calmed her, talking to her for several minutes. Poca was clearly frightened at first, but Manuel calmed her, his voice low, almost chanting to her. After a couple of minutes, she was relaxed, but he continued to talk to her for several more minutes. I was listening but couldn't understand a word of what he was saying. Finally, he rose from her neck and held the reins as Poca came to her feet. Then he stood next to her, still talking and stroking her neck and shoulders. His voice, in the smooth, relaxing chant of horse talk, continued as Manuel swung lightly into the saddle. The filly stood quietly for a few seconds and then, when Manuel touched her neck, stepped off quite naturally. Poca never offered to buck again the rest of her life. When I asked Manuel what he had said to her, he told me he had merely calmed her down. I think I knew enough to know that I was going to have to wait a few years to get to that lesson.

Four years later there was a knock on the door one evening while we were eating supper. When I answered it, there was Manuel, looking very worried. I invited him in and he came to the doorway between the kitchen and the breakfast room where he could talk to Daddy and Mamma.

"You need to call the vet," Manuel said, "the bay is sick."

"What's wrong with her?" Mamma asked.

"I don't know," Manuel replied, "but she's sick."

Manuel was someone to trust about recognizing horse ailments. If he didn't know what it was, we needed a vet.

When the vet arrived the next morning, he couldn't find

anything wrong with Poca but he took a blood sample with him when he left. He called later to tell us the bad news. Poca had V.E.E., Venezuelan Equine Encephalitis, a disease few horses survive. I stayed with her as much as I could, but school took most of my time. Manuel nursed her through the critical period of the illness, staying with her constantly. When it was over and she was on the road to recover, the vet stopped by one day, supposedly to check on her, but mostly to ask a question.

"How did you know she was sick?" he asked Daddy. "It was at least another twenty-four hours after I saw her before she would have started manifesting any symptoms."

"Manuel knew," Daddy replied.

And the vet left, knowing Manuel well enough to accept the explanation. Mamma wanted to know, though, so she asked Manuel.

"Oh, Miz Garry," Manuel said, "her eyes were so sad."

That was enough for Mamma, for all of us. Poca was not a sad horse and Manuel could hear what her eyes were saying.

Manuel spoke various animal languages far better than he spoke English, which was definitely a second and often very formal language for him. Though my Spanish was much worse than his English, I used a tape recorder at times and let him tell stories in Spanish that I could later struggle through translating. Generally, though, we spoke in English.

Manuel was born in Mexico in the shadow of a mountain called the Sleeping Lady. His family, as far back as he knew, had been on the same hacienda. He was, like his father and his father's father before him, a vaquero. He was *gente de campo*—of the land. He knew the *cabañuelas* method of predicting the weather, though he recognized it was no better than most others; he trusted his ability to read the clouds and the wind. And one evening, as we were finishing chores, I wondered out loud when the moon would rise the following Friday night, the night before deer season opened. I watched as Manuel calculated quietly to himself and then told me. I asked how he knew, and he replied, *la epacta.* When I pursued it, he explained that if you know the number of days past new that the moon is on the first day of the year you can calculate the date of each new moon of the year as long as you recall that the lunar year is eleven days short of the solar year. The rest was easy, since I already knew that the moon rises about fifty minutes later each night. I filed that one away as one of the many useful pieces of knowledge Manuel had given me, thinking nothing else of it, except to use it when I needed to. Until I was taking an archaeology course some years later, that is. One day the lecturer, talking about the calendar of Mayans, began to describe the long-lost but recently (in the last few years) discovered Mayan system for calculating the phases of the moon. As he described it, I realized that the Mayan system had not been lost but that the useful science of the aristocrats had passed on to and been preserved by the *gente de campo.* When next I was home, I asked Manuel where he had learned *la epacta.* He looked at me as though it were a strange question. Everyone knew *la epacta*—it was part of the texture of the land itself. So I left him, wondering about the discoveries of science and the knowledge of the land, about where and how they overlapped, and about wise old men.

By the time I was old enough to know that childhood was not the same the world over, I asked him what life had been like when he was a boy. He told me this story.

"This happened before the Revolution, when I was perhaps ten years old. That land hadn't changed since the hacienda had been established; that was two hundred years ago.

There were just a few roads and they were nothing more than wagon tracks. There were a few big towns, like Villa Acuña or Piedras Negras, along the River. Besides those towns that land had only small villages. And not many of them. There were no cars, no radio, nothing of modern times. It was a land of grass and bush. Good country for wild cattle and for vaqueros. That year I went for the first time on a big cattle gathering. I accompanied my father and an uncle. We began south of Nuevo Laredo and gathered cattle throughout a broad stretch of country on the Mexican side of the River all the way up past the mouth of the Pecos. I don't remember how wide the stretch was, but it was many miles. All the cattle of that area, vast as it was, were, like us, of our hacienda. My job was to help take care of the remuda and to do whatever was needed around the camp at night. I was proud to be included; it was the beginning of my work as a man.

"We would spend a few days gathering all the cattle in a place. Then we would take a day to work them. The mature steers we kept. We cut back the cows and calves so there would be more, next time. The bulls we left alone. They were so wild and had so much fighting blood in them that they would attack you, even when you were horseback. When we finished at one place, we drove the steers along to the next place and started over.

"After three or four months, we had reached the edge of the hacienda's range, west of the mouth of the Pecos. We swam the River there and drove the steers to Sanderson. Mr. John Blocker bought them. I think he shipped them to Kansas. We rode back down to Del Rio on the Texas side of the River and crossed on the bridge. We were paid when we got to Acuña. I was paid half what the men were, fifteen dollars for three months' work. My daddy wouldn't let me spend any of it in Acuña. He said we would need it later. But that didn't matter. When I rode into the hacienda with the remuda trailing me, I felt like a man—a vaquero.

"I loved working with the horses. There were hundreds of them on the hacienda: saddle horses, carriage horses, heavy draft horses. I loved them all. I trained them all. I would have stayed there forever. I would have been a vaquero like my father. But the Revolution came. It changed everything. The hacienda broke up. There was no work, no money. There was no difference between armies and bandit gangs. To ride a good horse was to invite robbery or murder. I rode a good horse. To protect myself and my horse at night, I would make a camp, cook and eat my supper, and then slip away. I would lead my horse for a ways and then stop and listen. Then I would ride another mile or two. Finally, I would stop and make camp again. I would light no fire and I would be very quiet. I would picket my horse to my wrist so no one could come up on us in the night and steal him. I slept with a pistol in my hand and my rifle next to me. It was no way to live. And I knew it would not change, not for a long time. So I crossed the River."

Manuel came legally. He went to work for a ranch near San Angelo. After a couple or three years to prove himself, he was put in charge of a little place the ranch owned: twenty-eight sections of land with twenty-eight windmills and not many cross fences. There were sheep on the place year-round, and they summered steers there as well. He had a little house, a set of corrals, and a horse trap in the center of the place. From there he rode all day, every day, checking windmills, fences and stock, and doctoring for screwworms, wool worms, and the like. Once a month, someone brought supplies, but generally Manuel wasn't around the house when the delivery was made. If he needed something—a windmill part, more fencing staples, whatever—he'd leave a note and the supply truck would leave it for him. Usually the only time he'd see other people was in the spring, when the crews came to work the sheep and to deliver the summer's steers, and in the fall, when they came to gather the steers and lambs for shipping.

Manuel didn't need much, and most of that he made himself. As I sit here writing, I'm sitting on the last surviving piece of the furniture he made for that little house. The seat is rawhide, as was the tabletop and the mattress. Manuel found all he needed on the land. When he told me that during those fourteen years he never once went into town, I was floored. I was a teenager then and pretty well fascinated with the bright lights, on an occasional basis. I asked him if he never wanted to go to town.

"I'd as soon go to prison as to San Angelo," he replied. I knew when he said it that he didn't mean anything about San Angelo in particular; he felt that way about towns, period. He wouldn't do his grocery shopping in Taylor because, with about eight thousand people then, it was too big.

After fourteen years, Manuel had saved up enough money to buy a little place of his own down at Carmine, near his kinfolks (and near us). During the drought in the fifties, he couldn't make it on his place and came to work for Daddy. When the drought ended, Manuel stayed. About a year before he died, Manuel had a heart attack and moved to a rest home. After a week or so, he asked my folks if he could come back to his little house on our place. When Mother asked him if he wasn't afraid of getting sick while living alone, he responded that Jesus could find him just as easily in the country as in town and he would be more comfortable waiting out on Brushy. I despair of learning to talk with animals as he did. But his teachings and his stories helped to keep me focused on the living world, and on horses.

Land and horses seem to be two threads running through my life. I was seven years old when Texas, my Shetland pony, died. Jimmie, my cousin who had "lent" me Texas, told me I could "borrow" another old retired horse of his called Mac. Daddy, Buz, and I drove the couple of hundred miles to Uncle James's ranch at Agua Dulce on a Friday afternoon when school turned out. It was an adventure for a seven-year-old: a long afternoon trip in the pickup, a look around the ranch the next morning, and then a really long trip home—a horse in the back of an old half-ton pickup is not conducive to speed. I was, of course, most excited by Mac, but meeting Jack Brown, Uncle James's foreman, wasn't much behind that. I'd heard stories of Jack from Daddy and Uncle James. I don't remember much about Jack from that first meeting, except that I was in awe of him. He looked like what a cowboy was supposed to look like, around six feet tall and as thin as a rail. His skin was tanned far beyond the stage where it might someday fade and was creased with lines that were the map of a life spent in the wind and sun. If his legs weren't bowed, they should have been. I was instructed to call him Mr. Brown, which I did until he told me otherwise, twenty-odd years later. I was fascinated with him; I wanted to know what sort of life he'd led to make him look like that. During my trips to Corpus and Agua Dulce over the next twenty-five or thirty years, I heard stories about Jack from Uncle James and Jimmie; from Jack's sons Jack Jr. and Jerry; and from Jack's own occasional comments.

Finally, a few years ago, Jack agreed to sit down and tell me his life's story. We sat in the ranch office for an entire afternoon. It was cool and shady in the office, one of the last days when the shade of two mesquite trees would be of much help as the South Texas spring slid into summer. Jack had time to sit and talk then; he'd retired and his son Jerry was foreman. Jack spoke around one of his perpetual cigarettes.

"I finished eighth grade at a little country school near San Saba and started working as a cowboy. My daddy was the foreman on the place where we lived and he wouldn't hire me, said it wasn't fair for me to go to work there, that I needed to get out and work for someone else. So I did, for a year or two. Then a buddy and I figured we'd better go see what some of the rest of the world looked like. We'd heard there was work for good cowboys in Arizona and we had a pretty good opinion of ourselves, as kids that age tend to. So we cinched our saddles around our bedrolls, threw them on a train, and climbed on after them. Several days and a thousand or so miles later we found ourselves sitting in a little cafe across the street from a train station in a little town in Arizona. This was as far as our money would get us and we were having a bowl of chili apiece and all the crackers and coffee they'd let us have since we were at the end of our string. We were discussing what to do next when a fellow stepped up behind us and asked if we belonged to the saddles and bedrolls out front. We said we did, and he said he was looking for hands and wanted to know if we were looking for work. We said yes and he allowed that he'd be back in an hour or so, for us to wait right there.

"We waited 'til he got back and realized that wherever we were going, we were taking a good 'eal of things with us. He was driving an old Model T truck with what I guess was the forerunner of a stock rack on it. Whatever it was, it was bulging along the sides with all manner of supplies. We tossed our bedrolls and saddles on top, next to his, and lashed everything down. By then it was getting on toward evening and we headed off into the rough country north of town. The sun set pretty quick and it seemed that the darker the night got, the rougher the road got until, probably around ten-thirty or eleven o'clock, it petered out altogether at a river. We dragged our bedrolls down and went to sleep. Along an hour or so before sunup we got up and built a fire and started fixing breakfast and unloading gear from the truck. While we were doing that, I could hear someone across the river getting up and catching horses. By the time we had breakfast ready it was getting light enough to see away from the fire. When I looked, there was a fellow crossing the river with a string of pack mules and some extra saddle horses. He joined us for a quick breakfast, and then we packed all the supplies on the mules, each of us saddled one of the extra horses, took a string of mules in tow, and headed for the ranch.

"It took all day going through some pretty rough country to get there. Along late in the afternoon we crossed a ridge and could see the ranch, tucked back against the farside of the valley we were looking down on. There were good corrals and barns, a long low-roofed bunkhouse, a cookhouse, and a stone ranch house. There were a series of big canyons running back out of the valley. We dropped down along the edge of one of those canyons and made it to the ranch in time to get everything unloaded and put away before supper. The boss told us to get a good night's sleep because we were going to start gathering cattle in the morning. I went to bed, full from a good supper, tired from a long day's work, and happy to be cowboying for what was clearly a sure-'nough cowboy outfit. Breakfast was at three-thirty, and by the time the sun was up enough to light the tops of the canyons we were riding along the rim of one. That particular canyon ran north and south and there wasn't much more than deep shadows down at the bottom. We'd been told to carry plenty of piggin' strings with us, so I figured we were out hunting cattle to catch, but I was puzzling over how the game worked when, watching the good open grasslands running back from the divides, trying to be the first to spot a bunch of cows, a big steer jumped up from under the little rimrock—it wasn't more than a couple of feet high along in there—and headed down the side of the canyon at a high lope. The boss called the name of one of the old hands and he hooked his spurs into his horse and they bailed off over the rimrock right on that old steer's tail. Pretty quicklike we lost sight of them but we could hear them tearing through the brush going down the canyon. The rest of us kept riding. I did more than listen, though; I got to thinking really hard about how steep those canyons were and how thick the brush was. Then there was the size of the steer I'd just seen, a mature animal as big as the horse I was riding, and I was giving some serious thought to the advisability of tying onto something like that on the side of a canyon like this. So I kinda eased my horse up next to the boss's and asked him exactly what the game was.

" 'When it gets to be your turn,' he says, 'I'll call your name. Just stay with the steer 'til you get to the bottom. It levels out down there and you'll have thirty, forty, maybe fifty yards of pretty flat ground to rope him and bust him. When you get him tied, just leave him there and catch up with us.'

"I waited a little bit for him to say more but realized finally that he had said all he planned to on the subject. I eased back away from him and got back as far as I could into the center of the group. Riders have a way of milling around as they're traveling through broken country, though, and before too long I found myself back up at the front of the group, next to the boss. About then a big steer jumped up, almost under my horse's hooves. The boss called my name and, without thinking, I hooked my spurs into the horse and we bailed off the rimrock, which along there had risen to three feet or more high, and away we went. Time we got to the bottom of the canyon I was not only still horseback but somehow still right on the steer's tail. I had my rope down and ready, which was good because there wasn't more than thirty yards of relatively level ground before it started to climb back up, and that side really was rough. I spilled the old steer and tied him without any trouble, that was the part of cowboying I'as good at, and started to pick my way back up the canyon wall to where the chase had started. By the time I'd caught up with the boss it was my turn again.

"I caught four steers that first day, and spent most of it either dreading what was coming or terrified when it got there. I rode with my feet kicked out of the stirrups so I'd fall clear of the wreck when it came. Of course, that old horse had grown up in that country and knew how to get around in those canyons. It was just that I hadn't learned to trust those horses yet. After supper, I managed to get the boss off by himself, where no one could hear what I had to say, and told him that I wasn't nearly as much cowboy as I claimed to be back in town and that maybe I couldn't handle this job.

" 'Hell, kid,' he laughed, 'you did fine today. You'll get used to it in a few days and it'll be all right. Besides, there ain't anybody going back to town for another month.'

"The next morning we left the place leading the same

number of mules as steers we'd caught the day before. Instead of heading up to high ground, we went up the floor of the canyon. Every time we came to a tied steer, we'd get ropes on it, let it up, and neck yoke it to one of the mules. Some of the steers were bigger than the mules, but the mules were all being fed corn back at the corrals and they were determined to return to the source of their grain. It might take a mule two or three days to get a steer back along a trail that it could walk alone in three or four hours. But the mules always got the steers back, occasionally, a bit tender along one side where the mule had made a definite impact on the steer during a particularly heated debate. Once all the mules had been hooked up and the steers were, reluctantly, headed back to the corrals, we headed back up onto the rims and started hunting steers again.

"The boss, of course, was right. At the end of the month when someone was going back to town again to get supplies I passed on the chance to quit. I was trusting the horses more by then and beginning to have a little faith in my own ability and judgment. I stayed for eighteen months, until we had cleaned all those big old mature steers out of the canyons and breaks. When we had them all, we drove the last bunch out along with all the mules and saddle horses and all our gear. The place was sold to some big money from back east."

I noticed that Jack had that middle-distance stare that I associate with seeing back over the years to a special time and a special place: that was when and where Jack had become a man. I asked him if he'd ever been back.

"No," he replied, slowly returning to the present. "The folks who bought it ran a road into it and fenced it; even brought in electricity. It wouldn't be the same." The word *ruined* hung, unspoken, in the air between us.

"After we got everything loaded onto the train and shipped out," Jack continued, lighting another cigarette, "the boss paid us off and we headed into town. It was my first trip to town since I'd gone to work for the outfit a year and a half earlier. I figured on going home but I couldn't get a train until the next day. I celebrated in the manner of many a true cowboy. I got a room at a hotel, had a bath and a haircut, bought a new shirt and a pair of Levi's, got a good steak dinner at the hotel dining room, then went upstairs and went to sleep between clean sheets. And I slept in the next morning. I didn't go down to breakfast until the sun was up.

"I had to change trains at a little burg out in West Texas a couple of days later. I'as sitting in a little cafe across the street from the station, having a bowl of chili, when a fellow steps up behind me and asks if I belong to the saddle and bedroll out front. I allowed that I did and he asked if I was looking for work. I said that I wasn't but he pushed a bit; said they just needed some help for a little while, that they were just gathering the pasture at their home place, that they were hard up and that there weren't any cowboys available around there, and that they'd be beholding and that they'd pay well if I'd help them out.

"I figured, 'How much time could it take to gather a pasture? What's another couple of days?' So I said yes and he said to wait there and he'd be back in an hour or so to pick me up. When he got back, he was driving a Model T pickup piled pretty high with supplies. I did notice that he didn't have a saddle and bedroll along or I might have gotten skittish. We got out to the place just as it was coming dark but still light enough for me to see a pretty good sized remuda in the corral and what appeared to be a chuck wagon parked behind the cookshack. But those were normal things to have around a ranch back then, so I didn't think too much about them until the next morning when I noticed that the chuck wagon was going with us and that we were taking the entire remuda along. The fellow I was riding alongside had worked for the outfit for several years, so I asked him just how big this pasture was that we were going to gather.

" 'Well,' he replied, establishing in my mind that cross fencing was a concept that had not invaded that part of the world, 'I don't really have any idea of the acreage, but if everything goes right, we can get it gathered in about six weeks.'

"I'd noticed that several hands had been assigned to keep a close eye on the remuda. That wasn't that unusual when you were leaving a ranch. There were always a few horses who'd rather hang around the barn and not go to work. They're kinda like people that way. But after what the old hand had told me, I started looking the horses over a bit more critically and, let me tell you, you didn't need to be an expert to tell that we were, that morning, riding about 90 percent of the broke horses in the outfit. I was beginning to have real reservations about eating in chili joints next to train stations.

"While we's nooning, it came out that I was something of a bronc rider and the boss of the outfit offers me five dollars a horse for riding out the rough string. What that meant was that at every horse switch I'd ride anything that a cowboy thought he couldn't handle until its fires had been banked a bit. I got the five dollars when a horse I'd been snapping the kinks out of came out of the rope corral and the cowboy said he thought he could handle him without my attentions first. Of course that meant that the gentle horses that were going to be really good someday were easy money, but the really bad ones that were, even in their prime, never going to amount to much more than canners, I got to ride a lot and might never get paid for. I was young, strong, and proud of my ability back then and, of course, there was the fact that a five dollar bill in those days was as big as a saddle blanket. I agreed to do it.

"By the time we got back to the headquarters, about a month and a half later, I'd forgiven the outfit for not being totally honest with me when they hired me. We got along well and it was a good outfit for taking care of its hands and its grass. They offered me a full-time job and even paid me for one old hammerhead that I'd ridden pretty nearly every day and that still wouldn't do for a working horse. But I was determined to go home and see my folks, so I bid them farewell and caught a ride back to town to find an eastbound train.

"I had one more train change on my way home. When I got off the train, I checked my bedroll and saddle at the baggage room at the station and walked uptown until I found a spot to eat that looked like it didn't cater to cowboys. And I ordered something other than chili to be on the safe side.

"It was good to get home and see my folks after being gone for the better part of two years. Of course after a while a visit wears thin and I started to think about getting work. I figured I hadn't really worn out my welcome in West Texas, so I headed back out there. Sure enough, the outfit I'd worked for gave me a job. I'd built myself a new bedroll while I'd been visiting my folks and I'd had the saddlemaker there in San Saba make a good working saddle, so I was pretty well set up when I got back out there.

"The first morning I'as on the place, we were running a bunch of horses in and one of them cut back and headed for the pasture. The foreman hollered at me to rope him, so I did. I'as on a good big stout horse and knew he wouldn't have any trouble with this old horse, so, when it came by me, I just dabbed one on him and turned that big old thing I'as riding off to take the shock. He took the shock fine. But the cinches on that brand-new saddle just weren't up to the job. They popped and I got a dandy bird's-eye view of the ranch headquarters. I felt like I went up thirty or forty feet, though it probably wasn't over six or eight, and the last thing I remember seeing before my head made contact with the ground was that horse. He hadn't really been running when I'd dropped that rope on him, but now he was flying like the hounds of hell were on his heels. In reality, I noticed, just before the lights went out, it wasn't the hounds at all, just my saddle bounding along through the rocks, the brush, and the dust cloud it and the horse were conspiring to make.

"We finally caught the horse about a week later, still dragging what was left of my saddle behind him. I put the remains into a to'e sack with a note that just had my name and address and the words 'Roped a horse' written on it. The saddlemaker sent me a new saddle and his apologies. I rode that one 'til it finally just wore out from old age. I'd've bought my next one from the same saddlemaker but old age had caught up with him too.

"I worked for that outfit for two or three years before I started to get homesick for the Hill Country. We'd shipped cattle and there weren't any horses that couldn't do without my expert attention for a while, so I told the boss I was going to quit and go see my folks. He didn't want me to. He'd've liked for me to have stayed and he told me so. But I was just as determined to leave, so we parted with his telling me that he'd never see me again but that my job was waiting whenever I showed up. I don't know what he knew that I didn't, because I fully expected to be back in the spring, ready to help with the branding. But after I'd been back at my folks' place for just a couple of weeks, I went into town one day and, walking down the street there on the square, I saw the most beautiful woman in the world and realized that I was going to have to marry her. The thought of marriage had never entered my head before that moment. But I not only thought about it then, I did it. And she's made me the happiest man in the world for the last fifty-three years. Of course my old outfit in West Texas was a sure-'nough bachelor cowboy outfit. There wasn't a woman on the place, never had been. I knew I'd have to find another place to work. But that was no problem. I started scouting around the Hill Country, close to home so my new bride wouldn't be too far from her family. It wasn't long before I met Mr. Jimmie, your uncle, and he was just setting up his place up there near Round Mountain. He hired me as his foreman and I stayed with him when he realized what most of the rest of us already knew; as much as he loved livestock and the land, he'd gotten asphalt and road dust in his blood. So when he started his own construction company down here at Corpus and found this place at Agua Dulce, we just naturally came along. Now, this old place wasn't much to look at then, just brush pastures without any buildings or pens, and the fences weren't much more than a rumor. I camped out here and oversaw all the fence work and the building of the house, barn, and corrals. Hell, I even helped with grubbing the mesquites. The day the cattle were delivered was, I swear, the scaredest I've ever been. More than that first morning hunting steers in the Arizona canyons. You see, the day before the cattle were to be delivered, Mr. Jimmie showed up and told me that he wouldn't be able to stay until they arrived.

" 'Mr. Jimmie,' I told him, 'they aren't going to unload those cows into these brushy pastures unless they have money in hand.'

" 'I know that, Jack,' he said. 'But it's all right. I've given you power of attorney. If the cattle meet with your approval, pay for them. Here's the checkbook.'

"When those cows arrived the next morning, I checked them over in detail before I let the truckers unload. They were just what we ordered, the perfect cows for that place. I was almost disappointed. It would have been so much easier to have been able to reject them and not to have to get that checkbook out. But, finally, I couldn't put it off any longer. I had to pay for the cows. I don't think I'd ever been called on to write down that big a number since I'd left school, thirty or so years earlier. I reread that check several times and counted the zeros several times. I reckon we'd still be there if the head truck driver hadn't've had quicker hands than I did. About the fifth or sixth time that I started to hand it to him and then to jerk it back and count the zeros again he grabbed it away from me and climbed back into his truck, muttering something about cowboys I couldn't really hear.

"Those were good cows. Mr. Jimmie and I did okay. Now Little Jimmie has the place and Jerry is his foreman. The cows are better, all registered now. I guess that's the way the world is supposed to work, things should get better. Nowadays I fish some, play with my grandkids, and come over here to poke around. I don't really have any work to do, but it's just hard to stop. I've been cowboying and ranching all my life; I just need to be around stock and good grass."

I knew what Jack meant. I'd traveled quite a bit by then, the land always drawing me on. Sometimes, like Jack, I go somewhere on purpose. Other times a piece of country just ambushes me. The traveling started in the late summer of '65 when I headed for Ann Arbor intent on a degree in wildlife biology. There I was stuck in a town for the first time in my life. Going to college isn't exactly living in a town—a college student body is too fluid to be a community. But I was on concrete five or six days a week. Weekends were important as land time: I got into the woods, either working on the student logging crew or with various wildlife research projects, just about every weekend. As a sophomore, I joined the Society of Les Voyageurs, a group united by wilderness-related fields of study. The L.V.'s, in addition to giving me a history of place (the society was started early in the century), gave me access to canoes and a house, the Cabin, with a park on three sides and a river on the fourth. Still, I was in a town. Summers became critical for me—three months on the land, far from any town. For all or part of four summers I worked for Texas Parks and Wildlife. I'd loved the Texas Hill Country since my early childhood; being headquartered there was like dying and going to heaven. It also taught me that heaven was a much bigger place than I had realized, for I spent time in West Texas working in the Big Bend and Davis Mountain country of Uncle Dud's stories. I also developed a case of desert fever that I still have. And I began to stand on my tiptoes a good 'eal, trying to look over the horizon, and generally facing west.

TRIANGLE X

━━◆◆◆━━

By all rights I should have spent the summer of 1969 sweating, literally and figuratively, through classes in Ann Arbor. But my departmental chair, Fred Smith, knew me well enough to know that I needed open space more than biostat or systematics. He told me to head west, to look over some of the country I might find myself working in when— if—I got my degree, and to clear my head before the fall semester. I was back down in the basement, sitting in my office with visions of vast plains, deep canyons, and high mountains swimming in the infinite space between my eyes and the pages of *Techniques of Wildlife Management*, when John Turner walked in. I didn't even look up, just handed him a pencil (John borrowed pencils on a regular basis), but he laughed and asked me what I was planning to do that summer. It seems he had some research work on tap during May (our semester ended the last week of April) and needed a hand. He wondered if I was interested. John lived on a ranch–dude ranch in Jackson Hole, Wyoming, in the boundaries of Grand Teton National Park. His research was with eagles and ospreys. I allowed that I didn't have anything pressing, just a tour through the West designed to get me back to Brushy Creek in time to turn the Jeep back north to Ann Arbor. A month or six weeks in Jackson Hole and Yellowstone sounded like a great way to start my summer travels. Besides, John and Mary Kay were getting married that spring and I knew he could use the help to get his research finished in time for the wedding.

So it was that on the fifth morning in May of 1969, I drove, my Jeep following John's station wagon, over Togwotee Pass and into Davey Jackson's Hole. Spring had come early that year and when I pulled off the road next to a big Doug Fir to keep from driving off the road I was lost in color: forty shades of green, blue, gray, and even more brown, all set off by the pure white of the Tetons, still winter-wrapped with snow, though spring had arrived in the Valley. But there was more: a taste in the air of wilderness. We had camped late the night before, at the Audubon Camp above Dubois, and had been awakened in the predawn twilight by the wind rip of duck wings above Torrey Lake. I had lain in my bag watching a moose in the willows across the creek and some of the Whiskey Mountain bighorns on the slopes above. Now, on Togwotee Pass, I was looking at one of the world's most beautiful valleys and sensing wilderness that stretched from here northward, clear up into Montana and southward to the South Pass on the Oregon Trail. I fleetingly thought that the three Tetons might be the Yegua Knobs— the three mystical hills that were a constant allurement on my personal horizon—as I climbed back into my Jeep and followed John to his ranch.

The Triangle X was, I saw as we turned off the highway and up to the headquarters, all native wood: buck-and-rail fences, pole corrals, and log buildings. The main house and barn I recognized from some old Western movies. The corrals were drying out and smelled of horses, a smell I missed in Ann Arbor. All of it felt good and comfortable and solidly western, something I desperately needed after nine months in an eastern town (everything east of the Mississippi, even the Great Lake states that refer to themselves as midwestern, is eastern to old Texian stock. But through that morning I was looking over shoulders: either back over my own, or past the head of whoever I was speaking to. The Valley drew my eyes and my ears. The ranch buildings perched on the East Bench, below the Mount Leidy Highlands. A mile below, where the Snake River flowed in braided channels lined with willow, cottonwood, and aspen, I could hear sandhill cranes. Beyond, the river terraces rose, ending in Timbered Island, the terminal moraine of the last big glacier in the Valley. And beyond it, seemingly perched on the far edge of everything were the Tetons, so white against the spring sky that they dominated the view even when you faced the other way. As I visited with the ranch people, I realized that I had not only come into a natural wonderland but stumbled onto people who knew this land and its history intimately.

We arrived at the ranch early and met Ike, the ranch foreman, just as he was getting ready to feed the horses. I offered to help. We'd fed probably half a wagon of hay, Ike driving the tractor and me on the back of the trailer breaking up the bales and kicking the blocks off to the gathering horses, when he suddenly wheeled in his seat and looked back, obviously expecting to see baling wire scattered behind us with all the hay. I didn't understand it at the time; I was rolling and wrapping eight or ten pieces of wire as Ike's expression relaxed. It wasn't until later that I came to know that dude ranches attract a good bit of help that doesn't know sic 'em about any aspect of handling stock.

When he saw me acting like someone who had been around enough stock to know that horses can't digest baling wire, Ike decided that I was, if not a great hand, at least educable. I guess we were friends from then on, even if, over the next several years, I offered Ike plenty of evidence that though well started I had much to learn about working in the mountains.

We had reloaded the hay wagon for the next day before heading back to the barn, so as we came around the corner of the barn I was on top of the haystack, ten or twelve feet off the ground, when I saw what I at first took to be a retired grizzly bear coming toward us. A second look proved it to be a man, big in his prime but gone grand of girth with age. He walked in a bearlike shamble that, like a bear's, moved him far faster than it appeared. When he looked up to speak to Ike, I saw, under his hat, tufts of white hair sticking out from behind ears the size of Lyndon Johnson's and a great white walrus mustache heavily stained by tobacco smoke and juice. As he reached for his snoose can, the image of an old bear was complete. His left hand looked like a bear's paw that had been pulled out of a trap; only his little finger and thumb remained. The other three fingers were cut off flush at the hand. Then he looked up and nodded good morning to me with a pair of eyes the likes of which I associate with long years staring over vast distances. I had already placed him from some of John's stories as Bill Daniels. I hadn't realized, as we nodded at each other in greeting, that that gesture was the beginning of a friendship that would last for years rather than days. But then I hadn't realized that the six weeks I was planning on staying was going to stretch into six years.

Within a week, I had fallen under the spell of the Yellowstone Country: the Valley, the River, the Hills, the Plateau—all spoken of without prefixes but all obviously capitalized when you heard people use the words, the exact river or mountain range indicated through context or by a nod of the head. John's research kept us busy three or four days a week, days spent chasing all over the Valley and Yellowstone Park, checking the reproductive success of eagle and osprey that had been exposed to significant doses of DDT. The rest of the time I just naturally fell into the routine of ranch life. We trucked horses back from winter range over at Kinnear, cleaned and repaired saddles and tack, fed (the Valley can't really support stock until pretty late in the season), and did all the other little things that need doing in the spring. I was also discovering the advantage of working for room and board: I didn't have to work full time. I was able to take a few hours each day I was at the ranch to ride, learn the country, watch the critters. Back in those days the spring elk migration crossed along the River in front of the ranch; on a couple or three hours' ride, I might see two or three hundred elk across the River, as well as moose, ducks, geese, trumpeter swans, redtails, eagles, and ospreys. There were beaver ponds, teepee rings, ancient campsites along fossil river channels, the remnants of an old placer mining claim, and a homestead. On those rides I realized that ravens are the wilderness birds that crows want to be when they grow up, the way kids want to grow up to be cowboys. And my eyes were drawn around to the subtle, hidden Absarokas—the vast wilderness to the northeast butted up against and spilling into Yellowstone Park. Wanting to know them, I turned to Bill. Every day, either right after we finished feeding or right after dinner, I'd head up to Bill's little trailer.

Bill's trailer was an old forties-vintage model that seemingly was designed by the same folks who design small blue-water sailboats; everything fitted into something else. Once your nose had adjusted to it, it was one of the world's most wonderful boar's nests. The coffeepot was always on for any adult visitors, and a big bowl of hard candy for the ranch kids rested on the table. There was an old record player and tottering stacks of records mixed in with equally tottering piles of books and magazines. Bill's easel sat in the middle of those piles. There were paintings and photographs, all Bill's work, stuck everywhere. At times I speculated that the dishes that were permanently stacked in the sink had some historical significance and that Bill ate off of others. During the summer months, when I first started visiting Bill, the trailer was parked up in the shade of the trees east of the ranch buildings. During the winters, it was moved down into the sun behind the barn. The seasonal movement did nothing to rearrange the interior. I grew to love the place, mostly because there was always a story to hear.

I knew Bill's memory and sense of place was phenomenal from a story John had told me about a pack trip he and Bill had taken together two or three years earlier. John said they were heading along a hillside that had burned back in the late thirties. A thick layer of second-growth lodgepole pine, called doghair because of its thickness, had covered the slope. John was in the lead with four or five packhorses. Bill was following with about that many more. John looked back and saw Bill getting off his horse. Thinking that Bill had a pack slipping, John dismounted, checked his own packs, and went back to help Bill. But Bill wasn't with his horses.

"He was two or three hundred yards down the hill by the time I got there," John said, "rooting around in the duff under some of those young trees, and muttering to himself about getting old and forgetful. I asked him what we were looking for, but he just continued to kick around. In two or three minutes he found a heavy chain, ten or twelve feet long, and began cussing in earnest. He was raging about how no one had any respect for other people's property anymore.

"When I finally got him calmed down enough to talk coherently, he told me that he'd left a bear trap there the last time he'd been through there and now, when he came back to get it, someone had stolen it. The chain was the drag for it. Whoever had taken the trap had figured the chain was too much to pack out and cut it off. Finally, he ran out of breath and I could ask him when he'd left a bear trap there. 'I told you,' he replied, 'the last time I was in here.' I knew the trail we were on was little used, so I was puzzled as to when Bill had been in there. 'Yes,' I said, 'but when was that?' Bill studied for just a second or two, doing some math in his head, and then said, 'Nineteen thirty-two.'

"I was amazed," John said. "Bill hadn't been there in thirty-three years. A major forest fire had burned through seven years after he'd left the trap there. Second growth had completely changed the appearance of the area, and Bill had walked to within ten or fifteen feet of where the chain was lying before he started to look. My God, that old man has a sense of place. He knows these mountains like no one else."

I had already seen that part of Bill on a lesser scale. He painted landscapes from memory. I'd gotten used to seeing Bill sitting at his easel, with his back to the door, painting the Tetons. I hadn't had to look at too many of his paintings to realize that he could see the Tetons as clearly with his back turned to them as I could facing them.

"Bill," I asked one morning as we sat drinking coffee and visiting, "what brought you to this part of the world?" In bresponse he held up his left hand to show me his missing fingers.

"I was born in the Willamette Valley," Bill started. "One day, when I was six years old, my brother Larry and I were splitting firewood for the kitchen. Actually, since Larry was older, he was doing the splitting and I was carrying it to the kitchen. Our chopping block was a Doug fir stump about six or six and a half feet in diameter. I was leaning against it on the opposite side from Larry. He told me to get my hand off the stump because he might slip and accidently cut my fingers off. I just laughed at him and told him he couldn't reach across that stump if he tried. But he could. I don't think he meant to hit me but, stretched out that much, he didn't have much control. He took those three fingers off as slick as you please.

"I had to quit school and go to work in the woods after third grade. By the time I'as a teenager I'd worked my way up to a feller before I left logging and went to work in a shipyard down on the coast. I was doing pretty good there, had worked my way up to shipbuilder, when World War I started. We weren't in the war yet, and in the winter of nineteen fourteen and fifteen, it looked like we might not get into it. So I went to Canada to enlist in the Canadian Army. In spite of all my pleading they wouldn't take me because of my missing fingers. When I got back to the shipyard, my straw boss got to riding me about not being man enough to get into the army, so I quit and headed to Montana to become a cowboy."

Bill and the straw boss hadn't gotten along too well for some time, and Bill, in the process of resigning his position at the shipyard, completely rearranged the straw boss's rigging.

"I hit Montana in the spring of 1915 and signed on with a cattle drive moving a herd down into the Big Horn Basin. By the fall of the year I'd reached the southern end of the Basin, around Thermopolis, and I'd learned two things: that I was never going to make a living as a bronc rider, and that God had created mountains. I just moved up into the mountains and never really come out. For the next few years I spent the winters around Thermop and the rest of the year up in the Owl Creeks and Absarokas. Thermop was an interesting little burg back in those days. I pretty much headquartered at the old Stone Front barn—that was the livery stable. I did a good bit of freighting and that's where the teams for the freight outfit lived. I guess I spent a fair amount of time in the saloons too—when I was in town. Of course I wasn't in town much except during the winter. I remember one time, though. I was just coming through the door of one of the saloons. Now, remember, this was before Prohibition. The saloons still had swinging doors, free lunches, and open gambling. Like I said, I was just coming through the swinging doors, still had them in my hands, when I looked back in the back where the card tables were and I saw Jesse James stand up and reach under his coat for a gun. But he was a little slow. The fellow sitting across the table shot him. I found out later he was dead. But at that moment I realized that I wasn't nearly as thirsty as I thought I was. I just turned around and got out of there.

"This Jesse James wasn't any kin to the famous Jesse James. That Jesse James had been shot by Bob Ford back in the early eighties. But the one around there was cut out of a similar bolt, even if on a smaller pattern. I'd had a run-in with him another time. The ranch I'as working for had a couple of young horses missing, so I went hunting them. The thing was that where I found their tracks just outside the fence, there were the tracks of another horse and of a man. The man's tracks were around a couple of fence posts, like the fellow had pulled the staples out, let the fence down, and then put it back up after our horses were out. I followed the tracks over to James's place. Our horses were in the corral right at his house. I had halters with me, so I just caught them and started out with them when his wife came to the door and asked what I was doing. I told her and added that I'd trailed the horses here and knew what had happened but that I wouldn't say anything this time. With that, she stepped back and Jesse James stepped into the doorway. Someone had told me that he kept a Winchester next to the door. The way he was standing, I couldn't see his right arm, it was right where the rifle would be. So I just wheeled my horse broadside to him and stepped off so the horse was between us. I slipped my pistol out of the holster but didn't bring it into view. Instead, I told him to step clear of the door. He hesitated what seemed to me like a long time. I cocked my six-shooter and waited. Finally, he stepped outside, without the rifle, and I relaxed. I'd figured he'd have to kill the horse before he got me and that would leave me time for a clear shot. I didn't miss very often at that range. Still, I was glad when he decided he wasn't ready to try anything. I didn't want to have to kill a man when the only witnesses were his wife and kids. I'll tell you, though, I watched him pretty closely until I was well clear of there, and then I took those horses back to the ranch in quite a hurry.

"I never knew for sure but I heard he'd been caught cheating in the card game. Whatever it was, I figured the country wasn't a much worse place for his having been removed from it.

"Generally, though, I didn't turn back at the doors of a saloon. There was one time when maybe I should have. It was one of the winters when I was freighting. I'd make runs out to the ranches mostly. I ran an eight-up to either a sled or a wagon, depending on the snow. Sometimes I had enough cargo to hook up two rigs in tandem. It would get pretty cold up on one of those outfits, so I wore a full-length bearskin coat and buffalo mittens and cap with earflaps. With all of that on and a lap robe, I couldn't move too well, but my teams were well trained. I'd just wrap the reins around a post there next to me and run the team with voice commands. I did have a box of rocks set next to me. If one of the horses wasn't pulling his weight, I'd hit him on the rump with a rock when I hollered at him. That way I didn't have to hold reins and generally I didn't have to move at all. With a pan of hot coals on the floorboards under the lap robe, I could stay warm enough even when it got down to ten or fifteen below.

"One morning I had the team all hitched up, ready to leave, when someone came in and asked me if I was going out that day. When I inquired as to why I shouldn't, he informed me that it was fifty-two below. Well, I thought about that for a minute or two and then turned the horses back into the livery yard and repaired to the saloon to check and see just how much whiskey they had on hand. Three days later it hadn't warmed up any and I was still at the saloon. I was beginning to suspect that someone was distilling the stuff faster than I was drinking it. Finally, I gave up and went back home. When I woke up, the sun was up, it was up around fifteen below, and I went back to work.

Fortunately, I was on a sled and there was enough snow so that it didn't bump too much. I seriously considered giving up drinking. . . . But I got over that."

John and I finished his research on the first Saturday of June. That night, while we were all at the rodeo, Harold, John's brother who ran the pack-trip end of the dude-ranch business, told me that Tommy, Ike's son, was taking a pack trip in to work on some of the trails around hunting camp. The catch was that he was having to go in alone and that wasn't really safe, especially that early in the season. Harold asked me if I wouldn't like to take a little trip into the Absarokas before I left. I thought about all the stories I'd been hearing about the Absarokas and figured that everyone should have to go on at least one pack trip in his day, so I said sure.

Over the next ten days I contracted an incurable disease that I suspect Harold exposed me to without a second thought—I think he'd noticed my susceptibility. Ever since that trip, I have had wilderness disease. I'm all right as long as I can spend at least a couple of months every year in the Yellowstone Country or some comparable wilderness. Without that exposure each year, I'd doubtless experience the agony of withdrawal: irritability, shortness of vision, and an ever-increasing shortness of soul. Fortunately, in the twenty-five years since then I've always been able to have my annual dose. The thing was I didn't know I'd contracted it, at first.

Even though Tommy would probably have had an easier time without me along, by the time it was over we were working reasonably well together and enjoying each other's company. We got back to the ranch in time to turn the horses and mules into the corral and put our outfit away before supper, and I started thinking about leaving the Valley and continuing my travels, maybe heading for the slick-rock country of southern Utah and on down to the Grand Canyon. At supper we found out that while we were gone, Jimmy Guest had asked John if someone from the ranch could pack him into the Huckleberry Mountain area for his summer research. Harold asked Tommy and me if we were interested. When I jumped at the chance to go, I realized that something had happened. My plans to travel throughout the Southwest were put off, indefinitely; I knew I had contracted a virulent form of wilderness disease.

Within a month, I'd been on four pack trips, started running float trips on the Snake, and taken up participating in the weekly rodeo in Jackson. It was along about then that Bill decided that if I was going to hang around Wyoming, I needed a little broader education. One day, as he was trying to explain some of his theories of archaeology to me, he announced that he was going to show me some of the state. "We can leave on Sunday," he told me. "It shouldn't take more than a week or so."

The next Sunday morning, as I loaded my camp outfit and Bill's bedroll in the back of my Jeep, I noted that the bronc I'd drawn in the rodeo the night before made me very appreciative of Bill's stove-up old age.

We camped that night just below the old occupied cave site and petroglyph-covered cliff above Dinwoody Lake. Across the fire, Bill told me of his first trip to the area, in the late teens. By then he had crossed the Owl Creeks and made the Wind River side of those mountains his home. A Shoshoni he was cowboying with told him of the "picture cliff" and Bill had come to see it. Once he'd seen it, Bill had to know more about it. He got his friend to introduce him to a Shoshoni man reputed to be over one hundred years old, a keeper of stories and legends. With his friend translating, he asked the old man about the petroglyphs.

"We'as sitting at his kitchen table," Bill said. "He was so shrunken with age that we'd had to push the box of food I'd brought him as a gift for telling his stories to one side so we could see each other. When I asked him what the petroglyphs meant, he responded that he didn't know: 'My grandfather told me that his grandfather told him that those were the writings of the ancients. They were there when our ancestors arrived here.' That was all he could tell me about those writings, or whatever they are. He told me a good bit of other things, but his inability to tell me about those petroglyphs just made me more curious. I was determined to find out what I could about those ancient people who'd put them there."

So it was over a campfire, under the writings of the ancients, that I began to learn what happens when an uneducated but hungry mind is turned loose on a piece of country it has fallen in love with.

"Since there didn't seem to be anyone else to ask," Bill said, "I started asking myself who these people could have been. I looked at the country around this cave and figured that these folks couldn't have lived here full-time; there just wouldn't have been enough food. Even if there was more rain back then, there weren't any fewer rocks. There just couldn't have been that much growing here for them to harvest and, if there were enough of them to survive over a period of several generations, they would have chased the game out of here after a while.

"So I says to myself, 'Bill, if a group of people had to move, where would they have moved to from here?' Well, I figured if they lived in a cave here, they probably would like to live in caves wherever they were—I guess I'd heard the term "caveman" and figured that's who these people were. Many an evening I spent with maps or just with my images of the way this country was laid out. In my spare time I went hunting caves. I just figured out how far apart you'd need these to be, so that you wouldn't be hunting the same animals and picking the same plants you'd been working on in the last place, and how far you could go with old people and little babies. It took a while, but I found nine caves that showed signs of occupation. And there were petroglyphs everywhere. Here, up by Torrey Lake, over the other side of Thermop, just scattered all through this neck of the woods.

"I was getting more and more interested in archaeology, reading everything I could lay my hands on, and beginning to work with some archaeologists, packing them into sites and working with them when they excavated. But then I took a team in to one of my caves. They found a pile of chips where people had sat and made tools and arrowheads and whatever they needed from flint. Two of those idiots spent an entire day sifting through that pile and at supper that night they were going on about what great flint workers those people were. They had sifted through a pile four or five feet in diameter and two or three feet high and hadn't found a single broken point. There was nothing but flakes in that pile and these so-called experts couldn't talk about anything but how these people had worked that much flint without ruining even a single piece. I listened to that for a while and got to thinking, 'Bill, there never was anybody that good at chipping flint.' Finally, I got up and went over there to where the pile had been, picked up a double handful of rocks, and sat down there the way they did to work rock, with one leg folded up to make a workbench and the other straight out in front. I sat there for a few minutes and thought about what I would have been thinking if I'd been a flint knapper. I'd have been thinking that this was important work; that we needed all the arrowheads—or spear points or scrapers or whatever I was making—we could get out of each core. And I would have been thinking that I'd had to pack that core and as many more as I could carry on my back fifteen or twenty miles to get them here. Then I thought, 'Bill, if these were that important, what would you do if you ruined one; broke the tip off or whatever?' And I answered myself that I wouldn't just drop it. I'd get mad and I'd pitch it. So I took all those little rocks I had with me and I started pitching them away from me and watching where they landed. When I'd thrown all of them away, in every direction, I got up and walked around the circle where the rocks had fallen.

"When those archaeologists saw the bushel basket of broken points I found in that circle, they got mad at me and wouldn't include me in any of their discussions. I never took an archaeologist out after that and I never told anyone where those caves were."

"Where are they, Bill?" I asked.

"Naugh," he replied, "I still won't tell. You can figure it out like I did, if you just sit down with the maps and take the time in this country. I'm done with archaeologists. Except maybe for that fellow Frison down at Laramie. But, hell, he's really a rancher."

That night, with the moon shining on the picture cliff, I drifted off to the sound of drums and song, far distant, either in miles or years. I awoke with a fascination that has not yet left. I have found petroglyphs all over that end of the country, as Bill told me I would. I've looked not only all over the Yellowstone Country but all over the West. It's been a wonderful fascination. But I've also discovered that Bill was not completely honest about his never again dealing with archaeologists. Several years ago, while working at the Smithsonian's Anthropological Archives, I found that Bill had at his own expense photographed not only the Dinwoody petroglyphs but had mapped and photographed the Torrey Lake petroglyphs as well. He did, though, leave his nine caves to the mountains and to those who would look but, he hoped, not touch.

After breakfast beside the lake, we leisurely proceeded to Lander, where Bill introduced me to several old-timers and to my amazement and joy took me to the movies. We spent the night in town so that we could go to *How the West Was Won*. Fortunately, the folks sitting around us were as taken with Bill's commentary as I was. He pointed out not only the movie's good and bad interpretations of history but also—I hadn't then realized that Bill had worked on more than a few Hollywood films or that some of the wildlife films he'd made back in the thirties had won awards—on the style and tricks of filmmaking that had been used.

We'd had breakfast and were on the road by daylight the next morning headed for Independence Rock. Bill said it was time for me to see what the film was talking about. There were plenty of hills in sight, but Independence Rock sits off by itself, a huge granite dome out in the plains of the Sweetwater.

"The wagon trains tried to leave Independence, just west of St. Louis, as close to the first of April as they could," Bill said. "If they could get to here by the Fourth of July, they had a good chance of making it to Oregon or California in time to get set up for winter. The Independence name comes from the fact that folks tried to rest a few days here before heading up to South Pass. So they were here taking a break and could celebrate Independence Day here. One time a group of those pilgrims dug a hole and filled it with gunpowder. They put an anvil on top of it and touched that off as their fireworks display. Seems like a terrible waste of gunpowder, but I reckon those folks took the Fourth of July pretty seriously. Hell, their grandparents had fought the British."

All that explanation had come as we approached the rock. Once we were there, at the historical marker interpretive area next to the Rock, Bill became deeply serious. He climbed out of the Jeep, camera in hand and almost reverent.

"My daddy was here," Bill said quietly. "He told me one time that he carved his name on Independence Rock. I'm going to find it." By then I knew Bill well enough not to say anything about the fence around the site. I just followed him as we climbed it and started the search.

I'd gone back to the Jeep at noon and fixed sandwiches and returned with them to where Bill was reading names. He stopped long enough to eat but, uncharacteristically, not to talk. He finished his sandwich, took a long drink of water, and went back to looking. Three hours later he found it. He didn't say anything; he just stopped looking. I walked over to where he was kneeling, looked over his shoulder, and then left. I looked back from the base of the rock and saw him photograph the inscription. He stood up, looked at it awhile longer, and then climbed down. Neither of us said anything, we just walked back to the Jeep, got in, and drove away. All he said was turn left when we pulled out of the parking lot. We drove in silence for an hour.

That night we slept on the flank of the Wind River Range, looking down at South Pass and back up into the sweep of the Winds rising back toward the Yellowstone Country. Bill revived as we drove into South Pass City. The restoration work that has turned it into a wonderful historic site, with buildings that you can walk into and see the fixtures and furniture of the 1870s, hadn't been started then, and Bill explained what he knew of the town from conversations with the old-timers of his youth. From there we dropped back down into South Pass to stand beside the road, and tried to conceive of the importance of this broad, sweeping, sagebrush-covered pass over the mountains.

"Just past here," Bill said, his eyes once again taking on that hundred-year stare, "the trail forked. Folks who wanted to get rich quick turned left and took the trail to the California goldfields. Honest, working folks turned right and went to Oregon looking for farmland. My family was at least trying to be honest: They went to Oregon. That's how I came to be born in the Willamette Valley.

"People streamed through here during the 1850s. Think of it: fifty thousand folks a year. God, it must have been something to have been involved in."

We stood for a little longer, staring at the pass and the years. "Come on," Bill said, "I want to show you the Green River country." We climbed back into the Jeep and headed west. For three days we looked over the Red Desert; as far east as Baggs, where Bill showed me Butch Cassidy's house and the safest bank in the West—where the Hole-in-the-Wall Gang kept their money. For an afternoon we followed the Overland Stage road, returning to the highway at the remains of the Point of Rocks station. From there he took me to Expedition Island at Green River. At that point in my young life I knew next to nothing about the Colorado River system. Bill looked down the river with his strange I'm-here-too-late look. He would have loved to have been there with John Wesley Powell. He would have loved to have been there before the railroads and the highways, before all the people who dragged cars, radios, and TVs into that wild country. Bill wasn't a throwback. He was as fascinated with technology as he was with everything else. What I recognized in his look was that he had a sense of place, of where it all belonged. That look hooked me. This river and the lands it drained I was going to have to get to know. But later. We turned back to Rock Springs for the night.

Rock Springs in the late sixties was a town closed down. Stores were empty, cafes boarded up; the only bar Bill knew that was still open was less than half full and there wasn't a soul he recognized. His queries were met with the same answer every time: Everyone he asked about, his friends of fifteen years earlier, was dead. We got a room in one of the few old hotels that was still open, and Bill retired with a fresh bottle of Jim Beam and enough memories to share it with. I went for a long walk, not knowing that I was storing impressions to compare to the Rock Springs I would encounter a half dozen years later when its latest boom would spill it out into the surrounding desert. I returned to find the bottle empty and Bill sprawled across the bed. God, he could snore. I wasn't old enough then really to understand how he felt, but I knew he was hurting, feeling old and abandoned; the whiskey had been necessary for Bill that night. I got my bedroll out of the Jeep and threw it on the floor. I also opened the window; Bill's breath was peeling the paint off the ceiling.

To my amazement, Bill was up and ready to go at five o'clock. He did look a bit like he might bleed to death if he opened both eyes at once, but pancakes, eggs, bacon, hash browns, and eight or ten cups of coffee later we headed up Green River, and the mountains rising nearer and nearer seemed to help. Before too many miles had passed, Bill rediscovered his voice: he began to unfold the history of the region, from Shoshoni migrations to mountain man occupation and movements to later settlement patterns and the development of ranch communities. But as he talked, I sensed that he was talking so he wouldn't have to think about what he'd realized about his own mortality back in Rock Springs. We continued up Green River and over the Continental Divide at Union Pass. Snook Moore wasn't home, up there on the divide, but the fact that he was still alive let Bill know that he hadn't yet lost all of his old ties. We camped outside Dubois that night and the next morning Bill took me to his old homestead at Double Cabins in the mountains above Dubois. I knew that he and his brothers had homesteaded around there. I had already heard Bill's story of losing the place during the Depression when they couldn't pay the taxes—$15—on the place; there was no cash economy around there then. But I wasn't ready for the site until I saw it. It is an incredibly beautiful park. It was, though, a park in the mountains, eighty-five hundred feet above sea level. I knew enough history to know that to prove up a homestead it was necessary to farm it. This place had a twelve-hour frost-free growing season.

"Bill," I asked, "what did you grow on this place, to prove it up?"

"Grow on it?" he replied. "You couldn't raise hell on this place if you irrigated with whiskey. We sneaked over to Idaho and bought a bunch of potatoes—got them in the field, so we could dig them ourselves and leave plenty of dirt on them. We smuggled them through Dubois and then, a week or so later, brought them down into town and sold them. We lost money on the deal, but it was enough for us to be able to prove up our claim. We didn't want to farm. God, all three of us hated farming. We wanted a place to headquarter up in the Hills for hunting and trapping. We could stay up there all winter and use it as a base to work from. During the summers and falls, we had a place for our horses between pack trips. Those were good days. It was a good place. These are still good mountains."

We stayed there all day, mostly watching the light and shadows change and listening to the wind. That night Bill talked late about the good old days at Double Cabins. I felt that life was seeping back into Bill as he talked, for the stories were not only of the days of his youth; there were stories of the winter just past and stories of no time or place—stories that Bill figured I needed to hear. When we drove back in to the ranch the next day, I knew I'd been privileged to see that part of the world through the eyes of a curious, active mind that had been asking questions about it for over half a century. More important, I knew that Bill had decided not to die just yet, something I wasn't sure of back in Rock Springs.

That was the summer of Woodstock, but I spent those days in a more mystical place than anything created by the magical gathering in New York. I was up on the head of the Snake and across at Younts Peak, where the Yellowstone heads. In between I crossed Two Ocean Plateau and stood for the first time on Two Ocean Creek and threw a stick in just above where the creek, flowing directly down the Continental Divide, splits and becomes Atlantic Creek and Pacific Creek. To stand there watching a stick drift up to what looks at first glance to be an island but knowing that an inch difference to the right or the left means that, in theory at least, the stick will drift past either Fort Clatsop or New Orleans. To stand there is to know that there is a water route across the continent. Though it isn't what Lewis and Clark or all the other searchers expected, it is no less magical.

That summer, like all students' summers, drew to a close much more quickly than I'd hoped. I returned to Ann Arbor via Texas and entered into my last year of striving for my bachelor's degree. Nine months later, after assuring—or, perhaps, in their eyes threatening—my faculty advisers that I would indeed return for a sixth year if they didn't let me out, I graduated from the School of Natural Resources with a degree as a naturalist and my Jeep already packed and ready to head west. I had three months that I planned to spend mostly in the Absarokas before I had to report to Fort Belvoir, Virginia, to begin my military career.

After about three months in the service, as I was finishing up the Engineer Officers' Basic Course, the Army admitted that the recent budget cut Congress had dealt it meant that it couldn't pay most of us and kicked us into the Reserves. It was like having something between two years and the rest of our lives handed to us on a silver platter. I traded the jungles and rice paddies of Vietnam for the wilderness of northwestern Wyoming. So, aware of life and the need to nurture it, in January of '71 I returned to the Valley, knowing it could grow strong there.

Every morning when we finished feeding, Ike and I adjourned to Bill's trailer to drink coffee, thaw out, and listen to stories. Winter was quiet time; even Ike, whose work ethic was second to none, would take time for a second or even third cup of coffee and exchange stories before getting on with the day's work. It was during that first winter that I came to understand that Bill was a modern mountain man. He certainly wasn't the sort who'd dress up in buckskins and practice the archaic arts of the trappers of the early nineteenth century; but he had, a century after Davey Jackson, Bill Sublette, Jim Bridger, and their ilk, gone into the mountains to live. Bill had hunted, trapped, cowboyed, logged, worked for the Forest Service, and just lived in the mountains. He had a photographic memory for place and an eye that recorded even the most minute details. He not only loved the mountains, he learned them as few ever have.

Winters sometimes run together, but I remember it was the winter Tote, John and Mary Kay's first child, was a baby that I finally realized how tough Bill really was. One morning, after feeding, Bill told me of a sheep hunt that had gone awry.

"It was getting along in the fall and we hadn't laid in much meat for the winter," Bill started in. "I'd been hunting one old ram that I'd tried to get good pictures of all summer and hunted with a rifle in the fall. I'd never been able to get in position to get a shot at him and finally decided that I didn't really need his horns as much as we needed meat. So one morning I left our place there at Double Cabins intent on getting winter groceries rather than a trophy. I'd discussed my plans with Larry and Shorty (Bill's brothers) the night before, so they knew more or less where I'as planning to hunt.

"I'd gone maybe six or seven miles when, coming over a ridge I walked right into a bunch of sheep that were bedded down in a field of rocks that were about the same size and color as they were. They dropped down the ridge and came back into sight about two hundred yards out, going up the next ridge. I was sitting down and ready by then. I picked out a good-looking little ram back in the back of the bunch and popped him. I knew I'd hit him because he veered off from the bunch and crossed the ridge seventy-five yards below the others. He was running downhill like a wounded sheep while the rest had continued to run uphill, the natural thing for a healthy bighorn to do. By the time I walked over to where he'd crossed the ridge and looked down the far side he was dead. Shot through the heart, he'd run about a hundred yards from where I'd hit him. The catch was he'd managed to die about twenty feet below the ridgeline on what looked like a very mobile talus slope. But I figured that if the sheep hadn't started a landslide when he jumped down there, I wasn't likely to either. I guess it would have worked that way, except, when I jumped, I hooked my hip pocket on a rock and it threw me off balance. I hit just off to one side of the sheep and the whole hillside took off. When we got to the bottom, the sheep, since it was dead when the slide started, wasn't in any worse shape than it had been at the start. I was all right too, except that my right foot was pointed pretty nearly backward. After checking it carefully, I decided that it was only dislocated instead of broken. There were a couple of big boulders lying there, just about the right distance apart, so I wedged my foot in between them and then pushed back with my left foot until the right one popped back into place. I laced my boot up on it to hold it in place and got ready to head home. A little experimentation told me that I wasn't going to walk back to Double Cabins, even if I whittled myself a crutch. If I cut cross-country, I could hit a trail only about a half mile from where I was and then it wasn't but about five or six miles home. I figured I could crawl that before dark. I knew, though, that if I left that sheep for that long, the ravens and coyotes would work it over so much that it wouldn't be worth coming back for. So I went ahead and cleaned it and quartered it. Then I cut enough brush and little saplings to cover it and keep the ravens and coyotes off of it 'til I got back the next day.

"I'd only gone about four miles when I met Larry and Shorty coming out to look for me. Well, not really for me. They were riding and had packhorses but no saddle horse for me. I told them where the sheep was, and they asked me if my leg was broken. When I said no, it was *just* a dislocated ankle, they said good and went on to get the sheep, so they could get back home in time for supper.

"By the time we'd finished supper my knees were really beginning to hurt; that was pretty rocky ground for serious crawling. You'd think that by then I'd have learned not to listen to Larry, but when he suggested I use some horse liniment on my knees, so they wouldn't be too stiff the next morning, I did. I guess it may have helped the stiffness, but there was gracious little skin left on my knees at that point and that liniment felt like I'd poured gasoline on my knees and then lit it. I think Larry knew that, but I managed not to say anything and so deprive him of any pleasure of seeing me hurt myself a second time that day."

That afternoon Bill spoiled a pool we had going on whether he'd lose his last four teeth before Tote grew that many. He went to town and had them pulled. When he got home, I asked how long it'd be before his false teeth were ready. "I'm not getting any," Bill replied. When I asked why not, especially since he'd worked for the Forest Service long enough to get the government to pay for them, he responded, "I don't reckon I'll live that much longer. I don't think the idea of the law was to make the government buy me teeth to be buried in."

The next morning I figured Bill would let us feed without his help. But as we pulled away from the barn, he came out of his trailer and climbed on the back of the sled with me. It was what he did then, not the story he'd told the day before, that made me realize how tough Bill really was. Everything he'd done to save the sheep meat and to get home he'd done because he'd had to. Maybe he could have abandoned the meat and poached a sheep but, still, he did that because he had to. That morning on the back of the hay sled I watched Bill stuff a quarter of a can of Copenhagen around the gaping hole where the dentist had removed his last two front teeth the day before. I shuddered in pain at the thought of tobacco juice inside those holes, attacking the exposed nerves. Bill just spit and commented that it must be cold since the stream of tobacco juice froze before it hit the ground.

When we got back to his trailer for coffee, Bill measured the icicles on my moustache (Bill's curiosity included the how and even the why of the fact that my handlebars would support so much longer icicles than his walrus would) and announced that these were the longest of the winter. Ike added that this was the coldest day of the winter so far—42 below. Since Bill had been to town the day before, the coffee had a little spice in it, so we had to sip slowly. That gave us time for the conversation to open up and stretch out some. Given the fact that we'd just been out for a couple of hours at 40 below, the talk turned to the weather and getting by in the winter. I asked Bill how he and the other trappers made it through the winters up in the Hills.

"It wasn't any trouble," Bill said, "as long as you were set up for it. During hunting season, we'd set up our camp-sites. We'd lash a ridgepole, twenty-five or thirty feet long, between two pretty good sized trees, and then lay saplings along it to make an A-frame. The whole thing was big enough that you could pitch an eight-by-ten or even a ten-by-twelve wall tent at one end. The tent flap opened into the center and you walled up the end of the A-frame behind the back wall of the tent. Of course you had to frame in around the stovepipe where it went through the saplings, so they wouldn't catch fire. Then you'd fill in most of the rest of the space under the A-frame with firewood. Along about the tail end of the hunting season, when it was time for the snow to start falling seriously, you'd cover the whole thing with fresh-cut boughs so the snow would pile up over it. By the time you came back in to trap it looked like a snowdrift with a stovepipe sticking out of it. The insulation was so good that, with the stove fired up, you could get the tent warm enough to get dough to rise for your bread.

"Now, when you went outside, stayin' warm was another matter. Oh, you could stay out overnight if you had to, if you could find some shelter from the wind, like a spruce tree that was drifted around, and enough firewood. But what we always did is set up several such camps, so that we could work a set of lines from each camp. We'd make a circle, staying at each camp for anywhere from a couple of days to a week. The good trapping was all in the woods, and as long as you stayed in the trees, out of the wind, you were okay. We never had a thermometer with us, but we must have been out quite a bit when it was this cold or colder. Only one time in all the winters I spent out in the mountains did I ever get into any trouble.

"You've been over the tops of the Absarokas during the summers: You know how quickly the weather can change. You'll be up there enjoying a warm, beautiful summer day when all of a sudden a wind will come up out of nowhere, clouds will form around you, and you're riding through a snowstorm. Well, it's worse than that in the winter.

"Larry and Shorty Flick and I were trapping together that winter. We'd been in one camp for about a week and it was time to pull out. The trail ran down one creek and up another, about ten miles. I had some work I wanted to finish before I took off, though, so I told Larry and Shorty that I'd meet them at our next camp that night. By the time I finished what I was doing it was getting on in the morning and, since it was January, the afternoons didn't amount to much. So I hit on the bright idea of shaving several miles off my trip by cutting over the top."

The Absarokas, for those of you who haven't spent much time in them, are the result of an extended period of vulcanism that laid down what is essentially a high, flat-topped plateau. Over the last fifty million years erosion, as well as deposition, has been at work. Because of that they look like other mountain ranges, but when you break out on top, instead of ridges and peaks you find broad flat mesas. Since the elevation is anywhere from ten to over twelve thousand feet above sea level, these tablelands are alpine tundra.

"Well, everything was fine when I got to the top," Bill went on. "There was no wind, and the snow was either swept off or packed so hard I didn't even need my webs. I was making pretty good time but the wind came up, strong and out of the north. By the time I'd gone too far to turn back I realized that I was chilling down way too much for safety. I still had well over a mile to go to where the trail dropped off the rim and I knew I wouldn't make it that far. There was a rim only about three or four hundred yards off to my right, but I had no idea what it was like. There are places up there where there's fifty or even a hundred feet of rimrock. If I got over there and couldn't get off, I was going to freeze to death for sure. But I said to myself, 'Bill, you're going to freeze to death if you don't go over there. You might as well die in a fall as from the cold.' When I got to the rim, I still didn't know what the edge was like. There was a cornice hanging out so far that I couldn't tell what was below.

"I guess you get pretty fatalistic at a time like that, so I just strapped my webs on and walked out onto that cornice and jumped up and down until it broke off. The fall wasn't that far, maybe twenty or thirty feet, but with that big cushion of snow under me I just sat back on my webs and waited. I hit on about a sixty percent slope and took off like I was on a bobsled. Hell, it was fun flying down that slope, going faster and faster, until it dawned on me that I was still going to be accelerating when I got to the timber. Luck was with me that day, though. I tore off the tops of several small trees that were sticking up through the snow. They slowed me down before I got to a big tree. And I was able to straddle it with my webs, so that I caught it with my arms and chest and didn't break a snowshoe. It did knock the wind out of me, though, and somehow my nose managed to hit the trunk or a limb or something." Given Bill's nose, it would have been more amazing if it hadn't gotten mixed up in the wreck, but I didn't say anything. "I got my wind back, picked myself up, and went on.

"Even with that little side trip, I'd managed to cut some distance off the hike, so I made it into camp not too long after dark. I didn't figure on saying anything, but something, maybe my nose being so swollen, tipped them off that all was not right with me. I told them that I thought I was getting a boil or something on it. I wasn't about to give them the pleasure of knowing what a damned fool I'd been."

It must have been a year or so after that that Bill became a filmmaker. He'd been lugging cameras around the mountains for several years. And I do mean lugging: he'd gotten ahold of an old Speed Graphic. For those of you who aren't camera buffs think back to the cameras newspaper photographers carry in old movies from the thirties and forties. To use one of those old, heavy cameras to do the kind of photography Bill was doing, a major tripod was a must. And the film isn't lightweight either. But he was serious about it and kept an extra packhorse to carry his photo gear.

It must have happened at Christmastime, when Bill and all the other trappers came down to Dubois to celebrate the holidays for ten days or two weeks. Bill told me that old man Fred Fish, whom he worked for a good bit, asked him one day what it would take for someone to make good wildlife movies.

"Well," Bill said, "I guess that kind of set me off. I'd been wanting to make natural-history films for several years. But I couldn't begin to afford the equipment, the film, or the processing. It made me furious. I'd never get the chance to make movies, and here was this rich man who had gotten interested, would buy the gear, use it a few times, then get tired of it, and it would sit around and gather dust. So I figured I'd just scare him off. I told him the names of the very best and the most expensive of everything. He wrote it all down and quizzed me some more about what it would cost, once you had all the equipment. Then he thanked me, bought me a drink, and I didn't see him again until the spring.

"I was working out there at the Circle Ranch" (Fred Fish's place) "that spring. Along about the time the grass was greening up in the mountains, Fred called me over to the main house one day. I walked in and there, piled up on the living room floor, was all the camera equipment I'd suggested he get.

" 'Bill,' old Fred says, 'here's all that damn camera gear. Get it out of my house and go make some movies.' I just stood there, dumbfounded. 'Well,' he said, beginning to get an edge in his voice, 'what's the matter?' I woke up real quickly then and got to moving before he could change his mind. As I was hauling the last load out, Fred stuck an envelope on top of the pile. I clamped it down with my chin and went on back over to my cabin. When I looked in the envelope, I found a letter from Fred Fish to all the bankers around there extending me a line of credit to pay for film and processing. I hustled back over to the main house and found Fred. He just looked at me and said, 'Get out of here. Be back in the fall; I want to go hunting with you.' That's how I started making movies. Kept at it for several years; Fred supported me for a while and I supported myself for a while. The Depression finally ended my filmmaking, like it ended so much else. I was able to keep taking stills, though. I wound up with over five thousand negatives after I edited the collection."

"What did you do with those negatives?" I asked.

"I gave them to the county historical society," Bill replied.

When I inquired about the negatives some time later, I found out Bill had made his donation years earlier. No one knew who, in those days before the society had a center, had taken the pictures for safekeeping. Someday, in some attic or basement somewhere in Jackson, someone will be going through some old boxes her grandmother stuck in there years ago and a wonderful record of the mountains and the people of the mountains back in the twenties, thirties, and forties will surface. I just hope whoever it is will look at those boxes closely and realize what she has.

When World War II started in Europe and Roosevelt began to prepare us for the war that we couldn't avoid, Bill found he was now an overaged man missing three fingers on his left hand. Most of the Forest Rangers were 1-A, though, and, as the military began to swell its ranks in preparation, the Forest Service found itself looking for people to fill out its ranks as rangers became soldiers. Bill figured that could be his contribution to the war effort: He went to work for the government. Thus began a love-hate relationship between Bill and the Forest Service that stretched well over fifteen years. There was no question of Bill doing the work required of him; he logged more miles horseback than any other ranger in that district, ever. He cleared trails, fought fires, patrolled the backcountry—his district would become a large part of the Teton Wilderness in later years—ran the elk feeding station at Black Rock during the winters and all the other things that were required back in those days when the Forest Service was way understaffed. Bill also built for the Forest Service. One winter I found a few feet of 16-millimeter film while searching for some other materials in a ranch attic. When we found a projector and looked at the film, it proved to be footage shot inside a plane as men parachuted bundles down into a meadow complex buried under several feet of snow. None of us recognized any of the men or, because of the limited field of view out the door, the landscape. I asked Bill about it and he said he had shot the film while they were dropping the building supplies that he wouldn't be able to pack in the next summer to construct a patrol cabin at Hawk's Rest. You don't need to know that part of the country to know where that cabin sits. The name tells you enough to see the place. Bill packed in the rest of the materials he needed the next summer and, in his spare time, built the cabin. He built it tucked back in the trees, out of sight but with a view to make any ranger remember what the Forest Service is there to protect.

When I asked Bill why he quit the Forest Service, he just said, "I got tired of trying to work with Rangers who couldn't recognize a tree until it had been converted into a book." Ike told me the story of the specific Ranger who couldn't recognize a tree.

"Bill had a horse, Red Cloud, that he thought the world of. The horse could get a bit ringy if you didn't handle him just right, but Bill always handled him just right. They'd sent this new young Ranger out to work with Bill. I think the supervisor's idea was that Bill would educate the guy, but the Ranger had just finished college, had a degree in forestry, and knew that Bill had only been through the third grade. He figured that he was Bill's boss and that Bill couldn't tell him anything. For someone who had educated himself like Bill had that didn't start them off on the right foot. And it went from bad to worse. Things had gotten pretty strained by the day the Ranger tried to unload Red Cloud out of a truck. He was trying to back Red Cloud and the horse wasn't sure of his footing. The Ranger choused Red Cloud and the horse reared up and hit a crossbar that was welded up across the top of the gate. It caught him just right at the back of the head and killed him instantly. When Bill found out about it, he just quit the Forest Service then and there. He just couldn't deal with an organization that would hire some idiot like that kid and put him in charge of someone who had been studying those mountains for nearly forty years. I figured it was the best thing Bill could have done—it kept him from killing that kid."

Bill left the Valley after that, went back over to the Dubois country, and worked his way down through the Winds. After several years, he'd wound up down in the Red Desert. By the late fifties he was herding sheep down near Rock Springs. The summer after John Turner died, his son John was eighteen years old and had to take on all of his father's pack trips. Louise, John's mother, was worried about him having all that to do without any help, so she wired Bill, who had guided for them some in the past, to see if he would come and help out. Louise said she never heard from Bill. But then about suppertime the evening before John's first pack trip was due to leave Bill drove up, pulling his old house trailer behind his pickup. He just pulled up and asked where he could park the trailer while he and John were in the Hills. Louise told him to park it down behind the barn. When I arrived, a decade later, it was still there. Back before FDR, when old cowboys—sheepherders, guides, whatever ranch employees there were—played out and couldn't really work anymore, they were faced with a destitute old age. The work hadn't paid enough for a cowboy to have set anything aside. So old-time ranches—ranches that were owned and run by people who were part of the culture rather than a corporation—took in the old-timers, gave them some little work to do so they could maintain their dignity, and made sure they had food, clothing, and a roof over their heads. A generation after Roosevelt started the New Deal programs, there wasn't much need for ranches to do that anymore. But some old ranchers and some old cowboys were still part of the old system. The Triangle X was such a place. After Bill got too old to stand the long hours in the saddle, the cold nights sleeping on the ground, and the work that had seemed easy forty years earlier, he stayed at Turners', did what work he could, but spent most of his time reading and painting; and educating people like me.

I had learned early in my career with Bill not to trust his pointing. For some reason he always pointed with his left hand, and since when he did he pointed with both his little finger and thumb, he got me lost several times. Finally, I learned that Bill's point had about a four- or five-canyon spread and knew to ask in a bit more detail where I was heading. But Bill always knew about something worth seeing. Once, when I was heading into the Washakie Range, an older mountain range buried by the Absarokas, I asked Bill if there was anything special I should look for.

"Three canyons back from where you'll camp," Bill told me, "there's an interesting formation on the left back up toward its head. It's up a ways, but climb up there and look at the black layer in the rocks. It's worth the climb."

I got back ten days later and, after the stock was back in the corrals and the tack was put away, I passed on a shower long enough to go up and visit Bill. He was leaning in the doorway watching me walk up.

"Did you look at that black layer I told you to?" he greeted me with.

"Yes," I replied. "Do you know what that was in the layer?"

"Sure I do. Those are Megaladon teeth."

"How did you identify them?"

"I dug a couple out back in the twenties and started sending them to people I'd run across at museums. Some guy at the Smithsonian identified them for me."

"More importantly," I asked, remembering that to reach the layer in question was just shy of a technical climb about 135 to 140 feet up the canyon wall, "why did you climb up there and look?" I'd done it because Bill had told me that there was something there worth the climb.

"I'd never seen a layer like that one anywhere else in those mountains. I just had to know what was there." And so I learned, fortunately, early in my time in the Absarokas, always to remember to question what I was looking at. Later, letting hot water soak ten days' trail dust off my body, I wondered how Bill had gotten into the head of a canyon that far off the trail. I remembered that he told me that for ten years, while he was making movies and taking pictures pretty much full-time, he had only gotten on trails to cross them. He had learned the mountains as few ever had or would.

Bill had given up filmmaking and only occasionally got his still camera out. He could no longer get around well enough to shoot the kind of pictures he always had. But his creative juices required some outlet, so he'd turned to painting in his old age. He was a primitive artist who understood the way moonlight plays on snow as well as any artist I've ever seen. One winter I noticed that Bill was painting almost the same scene over and over. The scene was of a tiny cabin, tucked back in the timber at the edge of a park in the high mountains. A midnight January or February full moon reflected off a recent snowfall that covered the trees and cabin roof and off of a thin stream of smoke that rose from the cabin's chimney. A faint light spilled from the cabin's window. A single set of snowshoe tracks ended where the snowshoes were stuck into a drift next to the cabin door. The thing that separated one painting from another was that the actual setting was different in each painting. The parks were real places up in the mountains; all of us who were looking at the paintings recognized the exact place where each cabin stood. After about the fourth or fifth painting, I asked Bill what he was doing.

"Well," he said, not interrupting his painting, "there were places that I always thought would be good places to have cabins for trapping ... or just for being there. I never got them all built. So I decided to build them this winter."

It was the last winter Bill had to build them. The next summer he had to have surgery; I think it was his gallbladder. He never woke up. I wasn't there when it happened, but Doc MacLeod told me that they scattered Bill's ashes over the area where the Owl Creeks and the Absarokas run together. There was really no place else for Bill to go. He had shared his life with those mountains—he should be there forever.

Bill had introduced me to what is now generally referred

to as the Greater Yellowstone Ecosystem. As I write now, I look up on my wall at a framed map of the area, stretching from South Pass northward through Wyoming to Montana's Bozeman Pass. East and west it reaches from the eastern edge of the Absarokas and the Owl Creek ranges in Wyoming westward to Greys Lake in Idaho and the Gravelly Mountains of Montana. There are stories that simply belong to the Land. There are others that are human and ancient. But there are too stories of people who have chosen, as Bill did, to live in this land that seems to many to be without human rewards. It is a land that has felt comparatively little human impact until recently. The history of this place is the story of relatively few people. Most of them are interesting: people whom stories grow around, people who tell the stories well. I spent six years working for the Triangle X, listening to all the stories I could. Some I went looking for, but some just showed up at the ranch.

Along the tail end of the summer of 1970, while I was gone for a soldier, the Triangle X bought out the old Teton Valley Ranch's pack outfit. For a full day the trucks ran back and forth delivering mules, bell mares, saddles, halters, pads, lead ropes, lash ropes, mantas, panniers—the whole shooting match. The next morning, when Harold Turner came in the main house for breakfast, he found Jack Davis sitting there. Jack had been the head packer for the TV for nearly thirty years, had raised and trained every one of the fifty-odd old TV mules and bell mares now standing in the Triangle X corrals. Here he was, Harold thought, an old man who, having had his life sold out from under him, was having trouble saying good-bye.

"Jack," Harold said, "maybe you'd better hang around a few days and educate us some about your old mules."

Jack looked up at Harold and said, in a voice that was stating simple, clear, unarguable fact, "Didn't Weenie tell you? When you bought them mules, you bought me too."

That was all that was ever said about it, all that could be said about it. Jack moved in and stayed the rest of his life. Well, the rest of his summers. Jack worked on the theory that the first snowflake of the fall that hit you was God's fault but the second one was your own fault. Jack went south for the winter.

That winter, while Jack was gone to Arizona, we built a new pack shed, nestled in between the stud pen and the loading chute, across from Ike's shop. It was eight big logs high at the eaves, thirty-six by eighteen, with a big porch along the long south wall. There were two doors opening onto the porch and windows looking out to the east and to the west. Inside there were racks for all the packsaddles, shelves for the saddle pads and mantas, hooks for all the ropes, and a loft to store tents and such. Along the west wall we put in a workbench to repair equipment and tack. While we were building it, we thought it was for all the packers. When Jack got back in the spring, it became clear that we had built it for him. Oh, he let the rest of us use it, but it was his. He put his war chest, filled with his tools, under the bench and set to work, rebuilding tack and fixing all the little things that constantly need fixing around a pack outfit.

There were several of us working for the Turners then, young and trying to learn our way around the mountains and the packing business. Jack became one of our mentors. (I reckon the old T X was a pretty good school—Tommy's now a ranch foreman, and H.A., Pres, and Bud all have their own ranches and outfitting businesses.) Having Jack as a mentor required some creativity. We had six weeks or two months around the ranch each spring between when Jack and the songbirds showed up and when we could get into the mountains. It was an ideal time to pick his brain and to get him to tell stories. But his work ethic was such that you couldn't just hang around and talk to him: If he was working, you'd better be working. So I'd go by the pack shed every night and haul off a few things—lead ropes, mantas, pads, whatever—and stash them down at the barn. The next day, when I had a few minutes, I'd stop by the barn, grab a rope or two, and return them to the pack shed. If Jack wasn't too busy, I'd ask him a question, something that would prompt a story. (I don't think I was the only one doing that; I noticed caches of pack equipment secreted in other places around the ranch.) When I went into the pack shed, if Jack was ready to talk, he'd stop what he was doing, reach under the workbench, and take "the black 'un," a quart bottle of Seagram's 7—a fresh one each day—out of his war chest and take a little pull on it. He'd offer me one and then put it away before repairing to the porch to sit in a sunny spot and warm up.

We sat in the sun on the porch one afternoon while I watched Jack fill, tamp, and light his battered old hooked-stemmed pipe. Once he had it lit, he puffed for the better part of a minute while those incredible blue eyes of his looked back through the years for the answer to my question. I had asked, rhetorically, I thought, how someone who hated cold weather as much as Jack had wound up in Jackson Hole. But Jack took it seriously, in a manner of speaking.

"I'as born under the Mogollon Rim, down in the Tonto Basin of Arizona," Jack started in. "The first four or five years of my life I just hung around the house and helped take care of the chickens and goats. After that, I started cowboying. By the time I'as a teenager we were getting pretty far along in a sure-'nough bad drought. I figured that I oughta take off, so there'd be more food for the little kids. I had a friend in the same shape, so we decided to throw in together and go see some of the world. We caught a bunch of wild mules, figuring we could sell them once we got them broke. We got them into a corral where we could rope and blindfold them. Once we had one tied up and blindfolded, we'd roach its mane, bell its tail, and fit it with a halter and a saddle. Now remember, we were kids and not as smart as we thought we were. When we had them all fitted, we roped and blindfolded all of them at once. We saddled and packed them good and tight and tied the lead rope of one into the tail of the one in front, figuring that the mule who was having its tail pulled would help to discipline the one behind it. We put them into two strings and each of us got on a big, stout, fast horse that we figured could outrun and outpull the mules. Between us we had enough little brothers to put one at each mule's head. We each took a lead rope and told our little brother that when we said the word to pull the blindfolds off the mules and to get out of the way. What neither of us had noticed was that we had one more little brother than we had mules. And he wanted something to do. When we gave the word and all the blindfolds came off, he opened the corral gate. When the dust settled, we were so far north of there that we just came on to Wyoming."

(On another occasion, when he was feeling a bit more serious, Jack told me that he had cowboyed around Arizona for several years after he left home, at about age fourteen, and didn't come into Jackson Hole for the first time until 1919. But who am I to worry about little details like that; the story's true if not necessarily factual.)

I figured that if the gate had been on the south side of

the corral instead of the north, Jack would have spent the rest of his life somewhere down in Mexico and I'd never have met him. Of course, Jack got to Mexico pretty regularly during the winters. All those years he'd worked for the TV Jack would, when the summer season ended, boss a horse drive from there to the Little Mountain country in the Red Desert of southwestern Wyoming. After the cavvy was located on its winter range and the cowboys were paid off, Jack would head south for the winter. Up into the early sixties Jack would take one or two of his best saddle horses, a good bell mare, and a small string of mules and head south.

Jack was a good hand and generally didn't have any trouble finding a job somewhere in the southwest or in northern Mexico, somewhere where the winters were as mild as the Wyoming summers. (Jack did tell me one time that 1936 was so cold he made it all the way to Guatemala before he warmed up.) One year he was a bit later than usual and was having trouble finding work. He had worked for the Chiricahua Cattle Company on a number of occasions and figured it was a good hole card; they would almost certainly have work for him. But when he got there, they didn't need any more cowboys. The boss told him that they could use him out at their horse outfit to help break horses.

"I had some suspicions about that," Jack said. "I'd worked for them enough to know what kind of horses they had. But I needed a job, so I said yes. Their horse camp was a day's ride from the headquarters, which might tell you something about their herd. They didn't want their cowboys even to see those horses until some of the rough edges had been knocked off.

"The horse camp wasn't much, a little cabin and a small barn next to a set of pens around a big round corral with a seven-foot-high stone wall. It set down along a little creek and, as I rode up, I could look down into the corrals and see the horses. They were all big, mature horses and all of them were only wearing one brand and it was fresh. I was looking at a bunch of horses that were anywhere from five to twelve years old and had just been caught for the first time. The outfit was paying me reasonably well, but, looking at those horses, I was beginning to doubt that it was enough. About then the bronc stomper came out of the cabin. He not only had to duck his head to get through the door but had to turn sideways to get his shoulders through. He looked big enough and tough enough to handle those horses. I began to speculate that maybe the winter wouldn't be as bad as I first thought.

"Back then quirts were as much a part of our gear as chaps and spurs. We wore them all the time, just hanging on our wrists. You'd see everything from a simple piece of latigo leather to elaborately braided, shot-loaded leather or rawhide ones. But I'd never seen one like what that bronc stomper was carrying. He had laced a leather thong, for a wrist strap, through the end of a couple of feet of trace chain. After we'd visited for a while, I asked him how long a quirt like that would last him. He smiled a lopsided embarrassed grin and said the last one had only lasted a couple of weeks. When I asked what happened to it, he said,

" 'Did you see that big blue roan when you rode up?'

"Of course I had; anyone would have. He was big, nearly seventeen hands, and there was white showing all around his eyes when he looked at you. When I'd come up over the rim and first looked down into the corral, he'd been watching me, like an elk.

" 'Yeah,' I said. 'Why?'

" 'He ate it.'

"I was six foot three when I got there that winter. When I headed north in the spring, I'd had my head driven into the ground so many times I was only six foot one."

I used to marvel at Jack, watching him move, or at least try to. Jack had been, in his day, a superbly athletic horseman. But by the time I came to know him he was an old man and incredibly stove up. Old cowboys are supposed to be stove up, but Jack was more crippled up than most. For good reason. We were talking one spring evening as I was putting my saddle away after running the horses down across the road. Jack had finished work and was sitting on the porch of the pack shed, having a nip and a little rest before heading over to the main house for supper. We got to talking about running horses and I showed him my overshoes that I'd peeled all the buckles off of that morning in a little bit of a high-speed horse wreck.

"Three of us were running wild horses down in Arizona one winter," Jack started. "We'd put a fence across a little side canyon to make a pen and got a pretty good bunch of horses into it. That was desert country and those horses were used to going to water every second or third day, so we held them there with no water for an extra day or two. That way when we turned them out, they'd have to head for water. When they came out of that side canyon, if we could turn them down the main canyon then the only place they could go to water was where we had built our working pens. To make sure they turned down the canyon, one of us had to get ahead of them to make sure they turned to the right rather than to the left, or up the canyon, where they could scatter and get away.

"I was riding a tough old hammerhead. He could fly, which I needed, but he was twelve years old and I was still using a snaffle bit on him. There was a juniper tree just before the mouth of a side canyon. To turn the horses to the right, I had to pass that tree on the left, between it and the canyon wall, to make sure I got to the upstream side of the main canyon and could turn everything down the canyon. There wasn't much room between the tree and the wall and a pretty good sized limb stuck out into the gap. There was maybe six inches between the top of the saddle horn and the limb, so when I went through that gap I had to lean off the left side of the horse to get under it.

"We jerked the fence down and everybody went for the main canyon at a run. I got in the lead and was feeling pretty good; that old horse could outrun anything else there. I guess I must have given him a little bit of slack in the reins when we went to the left of that tree 'cause he cut back to the right. It happened so quickly that, when he passed it on the right, I was still hanging down on his left side. I just kissed that juniper. When I came to, I was alone. I knew without anyone having to tell me that my jaw was broken, but it took a careful examination to know that, though most of them were loose, all my teeth were still in my mouth. Before I'd walked much more than a mile, I met my buddies coming back for me. They'd gotten the horses penned without any trouble. So I mounted up and we started back toward our camp at the working pens.

"I was just loafing around for a few days, being the cook and camp jack, letting my jaw heal. But several times a day I'd notice my legs would get all tingly like they had been asleep and the ache in my back that I'd had since the wreck didn't go away like I thought it should. I started getting a little nervous. Finally, after about three or four days, I went into town and had the doctor check my back. He threw me into the hospital, in traction; my back was broken. They kept me in there for nearly a month until it healed."

I asked Jack if they'd wired his jaw up too.

"Hell," he responded, "they weren't feeding me anything but soup and Jell-O anyway. I never told them my jaw was broken."

It's not unusual for a late-spring storm to hit Jackson Hole a week or so after everyone decides that summer has arrived. The first or even the second week of June, when the days are getting sure-'nough long and the sun can make you hot, a storm will slip up through Snake River Canyon or down off the Yellowstone Plateau. People have to dig out their winter coats again, and for two or three days everyone has to wear overshoes out in the corrals. The snow falls in clusters of flakes just shy of snowballs. Everything is damp and the dudes tend to hang around the fireplace at the main house, read, play cards, and visit. For Jack those few days were agony. He could barely move his old, battered, arthritic body around the ranch. Even the pack shed with its over-sized heater roaring full blast didn't seem to help.

One year, after a storm like that, the sun came out on the fourth day and summer seriously cranked up. I stopped by the pack shed about the middle of the morning and found Jack sitting on the porch. For him to be sitting there, alone, rather than to be in the shed working was indicative. He was soaking up the sun like a reptile. No fire smaller than the sun was going to thaw him out enough for his joints to bend with a manageable level of pain. The other indication was the "black 'un" sitting next to the chair. Jack didn't leave it out in the open, normally, but that day he needed it for its medicinal properties. I sat down on the porch, leaned against one of the roof pillars, and reflected on the fact that the sun did indeed feel good. Our conversation naturally drifted from storms into the aches and pains that come at the end of a life like Jack's. Finally, I asked him which pains of all the ones he'd had had been the worst. He didn't have to think at all. He held up his left hand, as much to look at it himself as for me to see it. I'd noticed before that the back of Jack's hand was dished in a bit and that he couldn't quite close his fist.

"That was the only time in my life I ever fooled with barbed wire, except to cut it," Jack said, shaking his head and putting his hand back in his lap. "Boyd Charter and I were building fence. Since both of us were getting a little long of tooth, he hired a bunch of high school kids to help with the heavy end of the job. There were two kids out front digging postholes. Boyd and I were coming along behind them with a wagonload of fence posts. The posts were cedar and had been cut with an axe, so that they were sharpened on the bottom. We'd take a post out of the wagon, drop it in the hole, and Boyd would hit it a couple of licks with a sledgehammer to set it. There were a couple of kids following us who filled the holes and tamped them. And there was a crew behind them stringing the wire.

"The only thing I had to do, other than to hold the post for Boyd, was to make sure that the kids digging the postholes were on line. The way I did it was to put my hand on top of the post sight between my center knuckles on a peak on the skyline. Then I could signal the diggers which way to move to stay on the line. I'd have sworn Boyd was finished setting that last post when I put my hand on it. But he took one more swing."

Jack held his hand back up and studied it for a few seconds. Then he took a little pull on the "black 'un" and changed the subject.

Boyd had moved away from the Valley to the Bull Mountains of Montana, so it was several years before I met him. One night when Boyd and I were talking about old times and old-timers in Jackson Hole Jack's name came up. I happened to mention that I knew Boyd had almost crippled Jack. He just laughed and shook his head.

"Ye gods, that old man was tough," Boyd started in. "I didn't see him put his hand up there, so I didn't pull up my swing at all. I pretty well buried Jack's hand in the top of that post. I lifted the hammer off and we both stood there for a few seconds. Then Jack reached up and kinda peeled his hand back out of the post and looked over the back of it, turned it around and studied the palm. Finishing that, he looked up at me and said, 'Boyd, I believe you have grievously injured me.' That was all he ever said about it. I know it hurt him, though: He drank a whole quart of whiskey on the way to town."

A year or so after Boyd told me what I thought was the rest of the story, I told it during a performance in Jackson, knowing that a good percentage of the audience had known Jack and would appreciate the story. After the show, Doc MacLeod came up and asked if I was interested in hearing what happened when Jack got to the hospital. Of course I was.

"I was working alone when they brought Jack in," Doc said. "I took one look at his hand and figured all I could do was cut it off and maybe that way prevent an infection from taking his whole arm or his life. But I knew that if I cut off Jack's hand, he'd kill me. So I prepped him. That is, I prepped him up to the point of giving him ether. Then I smelled the alcohol on his breath. 'Jack,' I asked him, 'how much whiskey did you drink?' When he told me a whole bottle, in probably a bit under a half hour, I knew I couldn't give him ether until at least most of it was out of his system; you just can't be sure how alcohol and ether will mix and I didn't want to have to worry about anything but that hand.

"If there's anything that will burn alcohol out of your system, it's pain. Since alcohol was his drug of choice, I figured I could start to work on him using it. In a few minutes, I reasoned, he would have metabolized enough of the alcohol that I could give him ether and really get to work. But as I got inside his hand and started working, I realized that the damage wasn't as bad as it initially appeared. Though most of the bones were broken, the ligaments and tendons were pretty much intact or could be repaired. I got busy sorting out which splinters were cedar and needed to be removed and which were bone and could be put back. I was concentrating on which tendon end to tie to which when my shoulders became so stiff that I had to straighten up and flex them some before I could go on. While I was stretching, I happened to look up at the wall clock. I'd been working on Jack for well over an hour. I'd figured fifteen, or twenty minutes at the most, would be enough to burn all the alcohol out of his system. He'd been lying there, with no painkiller at all for a long time, while I had been moving some big exposed nerves around in his hand. His face was soaked in sweat, but he never had flinched or said a word. 'Jack,' I asked, 'what say I give you a little something for the pain?' 'Doc,' he replied, 'I think I could use another drink.' I gave him something a bit stronger than whiskey, put him under, and finished working on his hand. Boyd wasn't kidding, that old man was tough."

Jack not only helped to teach a generation of young packers their business, he helped to pass on traditions and to tie us more directly into our heritage. His method would have done a Marine Corp D.I. proud. Jack had learned to pack as a kid from old men in Arizona. Those men and the *cargadors* who had taught them, going back to the days of the Spanish, had plied their trade in Apacharia. One of the realities of their lives was that the natives considered them hostile intruders; and vice versa. The most dangerous time of the day for an attack by Apaches was at first light. A camp asleep then, was a camp subject to attack. A wise packer in those days was up and ready at first light. Jack had been taught by wise packers; packers who lacked wisdom didn't tend to live long enough to teach. He had learned their wisdom and realized that even though we ran little risk of being attacked, we could utilize that much more of the day if we started a bit before the day did. Jack woke up with the morning star, dressed, and rolled his bedroll. Then he hollered to the camp, "Yea ho! Injuns! Almost daylight!" Then he repeated it. If you weren't up and moving by the time he finished the second time, he came over and stood on your bedroll, with his feet just above your shoulders so you couldn't get out. Then he'd reach down in after you, grab a handful of hair, and shake until you thought you were being scalped. When he let go, you were awake and moving at full speed. You tended not to try sleeping in more than once when you worked with Jack.

We all rolled out, dressed, and rolled our bedrolls. Then while the cook started the fires and began fixing breakfast, the wrangler went out after the horses. A couple of us would lay out the pack saddles in order, while someone went after the picketed bell mare. With her bell and nose bag leading the way, the mules came in to be caught, saddled, and tied to trees or hitch lines. By the time we were finished saddling, the cook would have breakfast ready and we could eat. By the time we'd finished eating, the wrangler would be bringing horses in. We'd go pack the mules while the wrangler ate breakfast. The kitchen mule was packed last, so that the cook had time to clean dishes. By the time the mules were packed and tied into strings and our horses caught and saddled the sun was coming up and we were on the trail, ready to start the day. The only difference between the way Jack taught us and the way Jack's teachers did it when they were young is that we usually didn't have to put sentries out around the camp. It was a good system that assured you wouldn't have trouble going to sleep at night and it only broke down once.

It was about midway through the first summer that Jack couldn't go to the Hills. He was finally just too stove up and in too much pain to put in the long days horseback. Dave, Ric, Tommy, and I were running his trips that year, packing kids into the wilderness for what had been the TV outfit. We had twelve five-day trips in July and twelve more in August, coming out the evening of the fifth day to camp at the trailhead and taking off with the next trip the following morning.

We'd had a little bit of a run-in with the Weber County Mounted Sheriff's Posse a trip or two before this one. They'd come up for a trail ride and had been misinformed that our pens at the trailhead were public corrals. They had parked horse and house trailers all around our corrals and had pitched tents in our hay yard. Jack arrived from the ranch an hour or so before we were due in. He had all our cargo for the next trip plus some clean clothes for us. When he saw our corrals, he almost had a stroke. The whole area was, to Jack's eye, pretty thoroughly trashed, behavior inappropriate anywhere but especially at the gateway to his mountains. Since no one was there—they were all out on the trail ride—Jack set about cleaning up. He hitched each of their trailers to his pickup and hauled them off a half mile or so into the sagebrush. Then he pulled down their tents and took them out there too. He had finished raking up the area and was burning the trash he'd found when the posse arrived. Not understanding their transgression, they were duly irate about the relocation of their campsite. Words were getting more than a little heated when we rode up. I never knew if it was the addition of four of Jack's friends or the fifteen ten-year-old witnesses we had with us that decided the thirty posse members to swallow their pride and to go camp in the sagebrush, but I was happy with the result. After supper, when the kids had left and Jack had gone back to the ranch, Dave told us he knew then that Jack was getting old.

"Even five years ago," Dave said, "Jack would have dragged the leader off his horse and clobbered him. Then we'd have all been in it."

We nodded, thankful for once of Jack's age. And we decided to take two-hour shifts on watch through the night, just in case there were any bad feelings over at the posse's camp.

After that trip, though, the summer had gone without a hitch. Our latest trip had been fine. The bus had been there to take the kids back to their camp, and Jack was waiting for us with the cargo for our next trip and a change of clothes for after our swim in Pacific Creek that passed as our almost-weekly bath. We visited some after supper and turned in by probably no later than ten o'clock. After what seemed like no more than a nap, I heard Jack's call and rolled out to start another day. Everyone said something about how short the night had seemed, but we caught and saddled the mules and then ate our breakfast. It was still pitch-dark night with no hint of gray yet in the east where there should have been good color already. We built up the fire for light and packed the mules. None of us owned a watch but we were, for the first time, beginning to doubt Jack's ability to read time by the stars. Finally, after saddling his horse, Tommy went over to his pickup and turned on the radio. After fiddling around with it for a little while, he found an Idaho station and discovered that it was a few minutes before three. Jack listened in disbelief. He swore he had seen the morning star rise. We had a good laugh at his expense, and headed down the vague outlines of the trail to the North Fork Meadows. Normally, we would arrive at the Meadows in time to set up camp before supper. That day we had dinner in the Meadows, set up camp, and had a nice, long nap before supper.

Five days later when we pulled back into the trailhead, Jack was waiting for us with a newspaper spread over the hood of his pickup and a look on his face that told us to hurry. I figured if World War III had started, there wouldn't have been any newspapers, but since I'd never seen or heard of Jack even looking at a newspaper, I figured for him to bring one out to us implied something just shy of war had happened in our absence. As quickly as we could get our packstrings tied, we assembled around Jack. The newspaper was opened to a small article in section B about a comet. The comet had developed a much larger tail than had been expected and had surprised astronomers by becoming visible to the naked eye just after midnight, Mountain Time, five nights earlier.

"It came up in the same place as the morning star," Jack said. "I stayed here and watched after you left."

I had realized, while thinking about the incident, that Jack did not have some magical internal clock set for the rising of the morning star. Rather, he woke many times during the night to listen for bells, to check the weather, and to look for the morning star. That night, after supper, I asked him if he always got up with the morning star.

"No," Jack responded. "When I'm at the ranch, I generally don't get up 'til it starts getting light. But in camp I learned long ago that it doesn't pay to sleep late.

"The first time I took a pack outfit from up here back down to Arizona, I'as lazing along, not in any particular rush. I camped one night just outside Moab, Utah, on a good piece of flat ground above a dry wash, not too far from the river. When the morning star came up, I saw the bell mare and mules were getting up and starting to graze. Since there was more grass there than anywhere else around, I figured I could sleep in 'til sunup and let them eat.

"Most people wake up when they hear bells. A packer wakes up when he doesn't hear them. Just about sunup I woke up when I didn't hear my bell mare. I stood right up in the middle of my bedroll and I guess I must have looked pretty puzzled, since my bell mare, mules, and saddle horse were all standing there grazing, right where they'd been when the morning star came up. I pulled on my jeans and boots and hustled over to see what was the matter with the bell mare's bell. It was missing. So was the picket rope from my saddle horse and the hobbles off the mules. I found tracks of someone wearing brogan shoes and followed them down into the draw but ran into some slickrock. You know, I wasted a few days going to school as a kid and that ruined me as a tracker, lost too much time. The Apache kids I grew up with who stayed out of school and worked at it could track an unshod mule over slickrock, but I lost that thief's tracks down there.

"I had to go into Moab to buy the leather and hardware I needed to build new gear. While I was there, I asked around to see if anybody might know anything about someone who was low enough to steal hobbles and bells. Folks were more than a little clannish down there back then and nobody seemed to know or care that he could have left me afoot. They didn't seem at all interested in helping an outsider. That was their mistake. You know the Apaches figured that anything they had was worth several of anything you had, so if you took something of theirs they'd take several somethings of yours. I guess it's the same thing bankers do: charge interest. Moab and I have had an Apache sort of relationship ever since. Every time I go through Moab, I take something. Sometimes it's nothing more than a candy bar, but it's always something. Those folks are never going to get through paying for my hobbles and bell. Since then, I've never slept in in camp. When the morning star gets up, so do I. That way I'm ready for whatever may happen before the day gets going. Besides, you don't waste any daylight that way."

"Yes," I thought, but didn't say out loud to Jack, "but you lose a good 'eal of daylight to an afternoon nap if you get up with a comet."

When I started packing with Jack, I realized that I had ridden past many of his camps and never known it. I hadn't seen his corrals, his fire circles; the grass wasn't beaten down, nothing. When I started working with him, I quickly learned how he did it. Camps were always set at the edge of a big park. The corrals were set back in the woods, where there was no grass. Its walls were either dead trees felled to interlock their tops or, when we were camping there, ropes stretched between trees. The gate was either poles lashed together or rope. Since the pen was in the edge of the trees, Jack could string wild-horse wings by running ropes out along the trees at the edge of the woods. Poles for tents and the cook fly were, when a camp was not in use, stood up next to tree trunks back in the woods to look like tree trunks. His fire pits were masterpieces of design. Blocks of sod were cut out and placed on a manta that was dragged into the shade. If the camp was used for several days, he would water the sod blocks. The pit area was big enough that a fire placed in the center wouldn't char the grass around the edge. When camp was pulled, all the wood in the fire was burned up, the ashes spread over the whole pit area and soaked with water. Then the sod blocks were replaced. Within a day, the fire site was only detectable if you were seriously looking for it.

Horses and mules were turned out, hobbled and belled as needed, so that they could scatter and wouldn't overgraze an area. One horse was picketed to a log so that it could move around and not beat up one area too much. That was the wrangle horse that was used to gather the rest of them in the morning. And horses were not only not allowed to come into camp along the same trail every time but were required to scatter and not all come in one behind the other, so that beaten paths wouldn't be made.

When Jack left a campsite, the only evidence was some mashed-down grass where people had slept and some piles of road apples. Even the road apples were something he would scatter if there were too many in one place. Believing in leaving as little evidence as possible of our presence in wilderness, I was impressed with Jack's system. But I didn't think anything about origins of the system until we branded colts one spring. We branded about half a dozen colts and, once we were done, he brought out a jar of some homemade concoction and rubbed it on the fresh brands. The brands healed up in less than half the time it normally took. When I asked him what it was, he told me it was a recipe that could get you in a lot of trouble. He wouldn't tell me what was in it. I'd heard stories that there were a couple of counties in Colorado that Jack wouldn't go into and that he may have had trouble reading brands during his youth. I'd never given the stories any credence, but adding that to his brand-healing concoction I asked him how he learned to hide camps like he did.

"Well," Jack replied, "let's just say that there were times in my life when it was better if nobody knew where my friends and I were camping."

I never pushed it any further than that. Everyone is entitled to a few secrets.

Jack came back to the Valley early one spring, in time to help us bring horses back from winter pasture. We'd finished trucking back from Kinnear and were preparing to run the horses back from the hayfields down by Mormon Row. It was only ten or fifteen miles across Antelope Flats, so we were just going to turn the horses out and chase them home. They knew where they were going, so it wasn't much to line them out and get them headed home, just an easy afternoon's work at an easy trot to slow lope made occasionally exciting by turning back the recalcitrants trying to take off for the tall timber of Mount Leidy.

"Jack," I said, "it's pretty tame compared to the old days (which had only ended a couple of years earlier), when it took you a month or so to gather horses off the Red Desert."

"Yeah," he responded. "But there were times when I'd gladly have settled for tame."

"Such as?" I asked, knowing we had at least a half hour before everyone would be ready to leave.

"April of '45," Jack began, "I and my sorta wife were coming up from Utah, where we'd put together a pretty nice little herd of horses and mules, all slicks (unbranded stock). They were all wild, but we'd had them together long enough that they were pretty well herd broken. We were up into the Red Desert the first part of April. There wasn't much there in those days, a few sheep outfits and the railroad, the Union Pacific. What roads there were weren't much more than a set of ruts. It was still pretty good wild country. Anyhow, we were making good enough time and everything was going all right. Then one morning it started raining; a cold driving rain that soaked everything. By noon there was snow mixed in with the rain and within an hour or so we were in a sure-'nough blizzard. Before long, the animals wouldn't go into the wind anymore. They started bunching up and turning tail to the wind. Pretty soon they started breaking and running from the storm. There was an old snow fence right near us and we crowded the pack outfit up behind it and started catching them and pulling their packs and saddles off. We got our tent up and ripped up a section of the snow fence for firewood, but I couldn't catch the young mule packing our kitchen outfit, which included a little sheepherder stove. He was so panicked by the storm that even though he wouldn't leave the bell mare, he wouldn't let me catch him. My sorta wife was afraid he'd really take off and leave us without a stove to warm the tent, cook some food, and dry our clothes, so she told me to shoot the mule. Hell, that was a good mule, I wasn't about to shoot it. Besides, I had the rifle packed on it. I had a nose bag, though, and that little mule finally let me catch it. I shot a horse late that night. It got down and couldn't get up and started thrashing around right in front of the tent. I opened the tent flap and took it out of its misery with the rifle. When the storm broke the next day and we looked out, there was a horse standing down at the end of the snow fence. He didn't look right and as I approached him I realized he had frozen to death standing up. Everything was snow covered as far as we could see. I figured we might have to hunker down for a few days until the weather warmed up and melted things off. But by the middle of the afternoon the bell mare, her mules, and a saddle horse had returned.

"There was a sheep outfit just about fifteen or twenty miles away, so we headed over there. My sorta wife hired on to cook for a while and I offered to take the kinks out of their cavvy. The rancher was glad for the help; this was all summer range and he was expecting to have to do everything for a while until the rest of his crew showed up in about three weeks. He got a pretty good cook out of the deal, and he sure got the kinks run out of his horses; I don't think he ever realized just how many kinks I took out of them.

"There was an abandoned set of pens down in the center of the country our horses were in, so I headquartered down there. When you're running wild horses, you have to keep on the move and you have to move fast, so I didn't take a bedroll or any kind of kitchen outfit. I left that sheep outfit with nothing but its cavvy and my saddle. I had one pocket of my saddlebags full of candy bars and the other full of cartridges for my rifle; that was all the outfit I took with me. I spent a couple of days getting the corrals fixed at the abandoned outfit and then I started hunting horses. That country was working alive with wild horses in those days, and wild studs had taken all my horses and mules into their bands.

"I'd spot some of my stock and then set after the band they were with. Sometimes I could cut them off, since they were used to being handled. Other times I'd have to crowd the whole band into a narrow spot and rope the one or two I wanted out of the bunch. And there were some of those studs that I wanted out of the bunch. And there were some of those studs that simply wouldn't let you take a mare from them. That's what the cartridges were for; sometimes I'd have to shoot the stud to get my animals back from him. Every time I'd catch something, whether it was a half dozen out of a bunch or just a single animal, I'd have to take them back to the pens and make sure everything was all right there. Then I'd take off after another bunch. It'd warmed up after that storm and I'd generally sleep during the middle of the day when I could stay warm in the sun. Nights I'd huddle around a little sagebrush fire and try to stay warm. I kept that up for about two weeks. I was just about played out by then, but I had all but one mare and her little mule colt caught. They were running with a stud not too far from my corrals, but he was sure-'nough skittish and I knew I'd never cut that mare off from his bunch. I was down to one candy bar and one bullet. I just wanted to get that mare, her colt, and go home. So I eased up on them, hoping to get close before they spotted me. But the wind switched and they winded me. We had a pretty good little chase then and I knew the horse I'as on wasn't going to last much longer. When the horses pulled up out of a draw a couple of hundred yards ahead of me and the stud came back to see what I was planning to do next, I just stepped off my horse, knelt down, drew a careful bead, and let a little daylight into him. The mares all milled around him and I was able to ride up, nice and slow, and slip a rope on my mare. She led easily, and her colt followed us back to the corrals.

"I held the horses in the corrals the rest of that day and all the next, without water. The next good water was back at the sheep outfit I'd come from, nearly forty miles away. I jumped those horses out as soon as it was light enough to see and fell in behind them with my rope in my hand. Anytime a horse slowed, I'd drag the end of my rope off its rump and hurry it up. When the horse I'as riding started playing out, I'd rope a fresh one and switch to it and keep going. We covered the whole distance at a hard trot to a run and, I'll tell you, when we got there, we were all ready to quit. Those horses hadn't had food or water for thirty-six hours and I'd eaten my last candy bar two days earlier.

"Everybody was happy. My sorta wife and I had gotten our horses and mules back and had picked up a little extra money, and the sheepman had eaten well for two weeks and had his horses ridden out, so they were ready for his herders.

"I used to love running wild horses when I'as younger," Jack ended. "I'd as soon do that as anything I've ever done. But that time almost cured me. I've just never seen any good come out of bad weather."

One morning in the spring of '74 Jack didn't come down to breakfast. When someone went up to check, he was too sick to get out of bed. Harold took him in to the hospital in Jackson, where he was diagnosed as suffering with cancer, far advanced and inoperable. The medicos said they could make him as comfortable as possible for the little time he had left. Jack informed them that he hadn't been born in a hospital and he didn't plan on dying in one. He came back to the ranch and did his best to live out his last days as he had his earlier ones. And he died in the sunlight, not in bed.

During three of the winters in the mid-seventies, I went back to Ann Arbor to get my master's degree. When I got back to the Valley in the spring of '75, I arrived at the ranch the same day my favorite minstrel, Singin' Sam Agins, did. I didn't have anything particularly pressing to do, so I took off with him to tour and entertain for the summer. Along about July a message caught up with me that my services, learned in graduate school, were needed by a citizen-rancher group called the Powder River Basin Resource Council. I agreed to go—for a year. Leaving the Valley wasn't easy, but it was time. I knew the world I needed to see was bigger and it was time for the next step.

So it was that on Labor Day I rode my thumb—I'd sold

my Jeep to cover a semester's tuition—into Sheridan. I was twenty-eight years old and for the first time in my life I was about to live in an urban community. I had spent my life trying to learn to listen to the wind, to read the land, to hear the stories of the country. Now, without a car to escape concrete and brick, I was a resident of a town.

MOST
ANY
MORNING
AT THE
RITZ

I spent my first day in Sheridan so buried in work and getting moved into a small apartment (I had to move the easy chair into the kitchen when I lowered the Murphy bed at night) that I didn't have time to think about where I was. But that night, as I lay in bed, I realized that I was living in a town. It was different from being a student. A student isn't really part of the town—besides, the LV Cabin, where I lived most of my years in Ann Arbor, was at the edge of town surrounded by a park and the Huron River, twenty minutes by canoe from a good marsh. Now, to do my work, I had to become a part of the community. I was, like it or not, an urban resident.

The next morning I awoke before daylight, which was my custom in the country, and realized that no one would be at the office for a couple or three hours. I got up and took a stroll around town, trying to get the lay of this—to a country boy—urban landscape. About six o'clock I was walking down Main Street, looking for a place to get a cup of coffee and read the morning paper. I noticed a sporting goods store across the street that had a number of cars parked in front of it. The Ritz seemed an unusual name for a sporting goods store, and that big a crowd at that time of the morning seemed a bit odd too, so I crossed the street to see what was going on. To my amazement, I saw a lunch counter inside. While I've never subscribed to the theory that a cafe where truckers eat has good food—most truckers I know won't eat a salad unless it's been deep-fried—the fact that there were plenty of locals at this place seemed a good recommendation, especially since the cafe across the street was empty (I later found that the coffee at that restaurant had a negative pH number). I walked into the Ritz and into a new phase of my life.

The Ritz wasn't like any sporting goods store I'd ever seen. Aside from the lunch counter there was, scattered in among the mounted heads and fish you'd expect in such a place, an antique gun collection of museum quality and pictures that were the work of a serious photographer rather than the typical hunting and fishing snapshots. Of course there was plenty of hunting, fishing, and camping gear, but it wasn't the focus of attention. It was clearly a place where everyone was welcome, whether the customer was ready to drop several hundred dollars on a new fly-fishing setup or was counting pennies to pay for his cup of coffee. I sat down at the counter and began to think maybe living in town offered some interesting possibilities.

Every day after that I showed up at the Ritz when it opened in the morning, sat quietly, drank my coffee, and listened to the stories up and down the counter. After about a week, I was reading my paper one morning when someone sat down next to me and spoke. I looked up into one of the most open, honest faces I've ever encountered. After a week of listening and observing, I knew that the name that went with the face was Sam and that he and his brother Paul owned and ran the Ritz. Sam was about my size and in far better shape than I associated with town dwellers who were pushing sixty. He introduced himself as Sam Mavrakis. I don't remember what we talked about; that wasn't important. What was important was that, by talking to me, Sam included me in the regular early morning "liars' hours."

The Ritz was my introduction to the haven that small-town cafes are. Often the tales were of the old days in and around Sheridan. I began to learn the history of this place I'd moved to. In learning about the community I also learned that the Ritz was, like Daddy's pickup, Bill's trailer, Jack's pack shed, a place to hear the stories that I loved. The greatest rule of collecting stories became clear: Go where the storytellers gather. For the first time I began to search for the tales rather than just being lucky enough to be around them. 'Most any morning at the Ritz I can listen to local history, military history, war stories, hunting and fishing tales, railroading stories, ranching and cowboying reminiscences, and bootlegging tales, as well as conversations on politics, current events, sports, or pretty nearly any other topic you can imagine. I have learned that the Ritz isn't unique. There are countless places to go to hear stories. Each of the great places, though, has, like the Ritz, certain qualities that make it special. Just in the northern part of Wyoming there are several such places: among others Lula Belle's in Gillette has the table of infinite wisdom, Buffalo's Busy Bee is still the place to hear Johnson County tales, and the Irma in Cody has a ninety-year heritage of stories begun by Buffalo Bill himself. Aside from being the only sporting goods store with a lunch counter, the Ritz has the Mavrakises.

Sheridan is a town anchored to the land: it is a ranch town, a mining town, a railroad town. But towns are, even when well connected to the land they sit on, centered on people. The Mavrakises are one of the families that Sheridan is anchored to. Sam in particular has always done what needed doing for the town, even when it cost money rather than made it. The Ritz is certainly not the focal point for the whole town; Sheridan is too big a town for any one place to be its center. But the Ritz is one of the first places people go when they need to get something done. And it is one of the places people go to relax, to visit with friends, and to get half a gallon of coffee for fifty cents.

The Ritz is a story in itself. There used to be a number of underground coal mines in the Sheridan area, put there to provide fuel for the railroad. Harry Mavrakis, Sam and Paul's father, came to Wyoming from Greece to work in those mines. When he was injured in the mines, Harry turned to running a pool hall and saloon. One led to two, as the saying goes, and Harry became a successful business-man. Mr. Volstead didn't hurt Harry's business overmuch. Actually, Prohibition helped because Harry was brewer, dis-tiller, and vintner as well as saloonkeeper. While the Roaring Twenties presented some problems for the Mavrakis family (the problems common to families involved in bootlegging), the family business prospered. Among other holdings, they had two establishments on Sheridan's Main Street. One, the Ritz, was a cafe and pool hall with some gambling tables in the back. Gambling was not necessarily legal in Wyoming in those days, but it wasn't really frowned on either. Just about every town had a gambling hall or two right in the middle of downtown, along with the saloons and houses of ill fame. Such establishments were simply fined each month. Owners, like Harry, paid the fines as a cost of doing business, no different from—indeed, no more expensive than—a license fee.

Harry's sons, Gus, Paul, and Sam, were athletes and sportsmen from their early childhoods. Sam, the most athletic, won a football scholarship to Brigham Young. I've never asked Sam if being the Greek Orthodox son of a saloon owner had any effect on his social life at BYU, but it certainly didn't affect his acceptance as a football player. Even back in the thirties, 165 pounds was light for a tackle, but even at that size he was good enough to make the all-American team his senior year.

World War II interrupted the Mavrakis boys' lives. When the war ended, Sam came home to a job offer from BYU, to coach freshman football. He jumped at the opportunity. Coaching agreed with him and he was good at it. No telling how Sam's life would have turned out if he'd kept coaching. But Harry needed assistance back in Sheridan and asked him to come home and help out for "just a little while." That was forty-some-odd years ago. Sam never quite got back to coaching.

It was during that immediate postwar period that Sam discovered one of the problems of growing up in a place where gambling was illegal but socially accepted. The story actually started back when Sam was in college. He was home for a visit when his daddy asked him to go down to the City Court to pay the Ritz's monthly fine. Sam got the money he needed and proceeded to the court. When his case came up, he said he looked around the room and he knew everyone in it. When the judge asked him his name, he told him. He pleaded guilty and paid the fine—he had the exact amount with him since the fine and court costs were always the same—and went back to the Ritz. Years later, after the War, Sam bought his first car, a surplus Jeep.

vhen he tried to buy insurance for it, Sam Rotellini, the
nce agent and his lifelong friend, told him he couldn't
n insurance because Sam was listed by the insurance
y as a known racketeer. That's when Sam found out
n you go to pay a fine, you use a fictitious name.

the saloons, or at least most of the saloon owners,
'rohibition. But the gambling halls of Wyoming
e it through the crackdown of the early fifties.
the gambling tables were closed down Sam and
run handling sporting goods in a small way
s tying flies for fishermen, and Paul was han-
t for the booming Little League craze. With
provided by the removal of the gaming ta-
led the amount of sporting goods they han-
d to another and within a few years, the
ced out the pool tables and most of the
ne that he'd watched people enter sport-
vously as salesmen swooped down on
ey. About half the time the customer
l any shred of ignorance. Sam said
relax and enjoy themselves at the
What better way than to keep the
stroke of genius. People do indeed
lunch counter helps, but it is the
o make everyone, from the queen
tpatients at the VA hospital, feel

t the Ritz once. It was in the
iting family in Big Horn while
she stopped by the Mercan-
e into Sheridan, where she
s the Ritz before going out
ral years before that, the

o
it
it
et
sh,
be
on't
r of
eally

have
d and
been
stood.
t's just
ow the
keteer."
rom Big
n, could
o would
consulted
ot it right:
a sporting

my job was

duke of Edinburgh had visited and gone fishing with Sam.
When he left, Sam had given him some flies that proved to
work well on Scottish salmon. The duke wrote to Sam several months before the visit, asked Sam if he could tie up a
few more flies for him and said that a member of the royal
family would be in Sheridan in the fall and could pick them
up. When Sam found out that the royal who was coming
was the queen, he wasn't sure that he, a "known racketeer,"
would be allowed to stay at the store when she came. N
one said anything about it—Sam certainly didn't bring
up—and the queen's visit went off without a hitch. The vi
was a week after the IRA had made an attempt on Marga
Thatcher, so the Secret Service agents, American and Brit
were more paranoid than normal; I don't say this to
derogatory, they get paid to be paranoid, though I d
think they get overtime for extra paranoia. The numb
guns and the amount of ammunition in the Ritz r
seemed to bother them.

After the queen left, a couple of the agents stayed to
a cup of coffee. They were considerably more relaxe
visited for a few minutes. Sam mentioned that he ha
afraid that his past would be discovered and misunde
"Oh, it was discovered," one of the agents said. "
that you have friends in high places. Friends who k
local history. We don't consider you much of a ra
I figured Malcolm Wallop was the friend. He's
Horn and, as a U.S. Senator and the queen's cous
probably qualify as a resident of high places wl
know Sam and the local history and who might be
by the British Secret Service. Whoever told them g
Sam isn't much of a racketeer. But he does run
goods store fit for a queen.

It is also a store ideal for my work. Part of

to keep my finger on the pulse of the community. The Ritz was the perfect place to supplement the knowledge I was acquiring from all the standard sources that I used much as a reporter would. As I became more integrated into the community and began to accept the fact that I was going to be living in town for at least a couple of years, the Ritz became almost as much a headquarters for me as the Powder River office. And quite a headquarters it was. If the Ritz had a time lock on the front door, none of the staff would have needed to show up when the place opened at 6 A. M. Everyone waiting for the doors to open knew how to turn on the lights, set the thermostat, turn on the coffeemaker, run the cash register, set out the doughnuts, etc., etc. The store's staff could have come in at seven-thirty or eight and everything would have been in order. I learned that not only was the early morning crowd made up of good storytellers, there were regular shift changes throughout the day. Once I'd learned the schedule, I knew when to get out of the office and down to the Ritz to hear a particular storyteller or a discussion on a particular topic. I also learned another reason that Paul and Sam were as well respected as they were. Among all the storytellers who frequented the Ritz, Sam and Paul were as good as any. For instance, one morning while Sam and I were talking, he nodded at an older gentleman sitting along the short leg of the counter.

"When Doc down there took early retirement," Sam told me, "it wasn't so he could spend more time with his wife. He swore he was going to go fishing every day. And for several years he was as good as his word. The thing was, Doc was a catch-and-release fisherman. That wasn't a problem on weekends, when his old fishing buddies could go with him. But five days a week he'd come in here and brag about the big fish he'd caught the day before. Truth be told, he was a pretty good fisherman. But nobody can catch big fish every day he's alone but not do any better than anyone else on the weekends.

"It wasn't too long before someone called him on it. He claimed he fished better when he wasn't distracted by other fishermen, but since he never had any fish to defend himself with, we all began to 'hurrah' him. He put up with it for a week or so, then showed up one morning with a Polaroid picture of a fish—a big fish. We could tell it was big because it was hanging on one of those scales that you can weigh and measure fish with. The tape was pulled out, so you could see the fish's length, as well as read the weight on the scale. Doc just passed the picture around and then told us to knock off our comments about his fishing abilities. And we had to. None of us wanted to admit that he was that good a fisherman, but every two or three days he'd bring in another picture of another big fish. He got to be something of a pain, really. It went on like that for several months. Until the baby came.

"Doc was fishing on a ranch out on Tongue River one day. The foreman came boiling up the ranch road a little before noon. He's trailing such a big rooster tail of dust behind his pickup that Doc knew something was wrong. The fellow pulled up next to Doc and hollered at him to get in. Seems as though the foreman and his wife were surprised to discover that their new baby was actually arriving a couple of weeks before they'd been told to expect it. The road out to the highway was about fourteen exceedingly rough miles and the foreman's wife said that if the two of them started down that road, there would be three of them by the time they got to the pavement. So the foreman had come for Doc. They hustled back up to the house, where Doc took charge of the situation and sent the husband off to boil water, the best way he could think of to keep him out of the way.

"The baby may have come a couple or three weeks before it was expected, but it was healthy. It may have been the first baby in Sheridan County delivered by a doctor wearing rubber boots rather than rubber gloves. Once the mother and baby were resting and the new grandmother had gotten there to help, Doc adjourned to the kitchen for a cup of coffee and a little rest. While Doc was drinking coffee and checking out the cookie jar, the foreman stopped boiling water, went into the living room, and took down the family Bible. He sat down at the dinner table to add the baby's name and the date to the family listing in the back of the Bible. As he prepared to write, he noticed that when Doc had dropped his fishing vest on the way to the bedroom his fish scale and tape had fallen out of its pocket. He looked at the scale and figured that he'd just weigh and measure the baby and record that along with its name.

"The foreman was in here a week or two later, bragging about how wonderful his new son was. I didn't think anything about that; every father thinks his baby is special. But when he got to bragging about how big the kid was, I was surprised and asked him if the baby hadn't been a couple of weeks early. He said, 'Yeah. But I measured him with that scale and tape of Doc's. He was eighteen pounds and almost thirty inches long.' "

One of the folks who laughed when Sam told that story was Herb Zingg. I figured his laughing was quite a compliment. Herb's a brand inspector, which means he gets to hear quite a few funny stories—not all meant to be funny when they're being told. Herb's always been good about pointing out good storytellers to me, telling me about someone I should look up and get to tell me a few stories. For instance, one morning at the Ritz the conversation had turned to broncs and bronc riders. When Herb's turn came, he told the following story.

"One time when I'as still a kid, maybe junior high school age, we'as working cattle down on the Middle Fork of Powder River. We wound up at those old pens at Kaycee. I'd been sent off on some errand or other and, when I'as walking back down one of the alleys, I heard a bronc grunting and bucking and a man laughing. When I looked around, I saw several fellows sitting on the fence at one of the bigger pens, hollering at what was clearly a bronc riding. Now, those were tall fences in those pens, but all of a sudden I saw the horse. I mean, I could see him above the top of the fence. He was bucking that high. And there was Bob Springfield sitting up there, spurring and laughing. That horse was throwing a walleyed fit and Springfield was enjoying it. That was the first time I ever saw Springfield. I didn't know who he was then but I knew he was a sure-'nough bronc rider.

"And he was a lot more than a bronc rider. He'd rodeoed, cowboyed, been a middleweight prizefighter, and had been in the army during the war. But mostly, he was a tribal policeman, and a pretty effective one. He was one of those who seemed to know how much force was needed to get a job done, even when the lawbreakers weren't exactly felons. One year—oh, this was years after I'd first met him, after I'd become a brand inspector—I wound up working at American Indian Days. I was one of the ones trying to keep kids from sneaking onto the grounds without paying. It was, I had decided, an impossible task. There were two of us patrolling a stretch of fence that was keeping kids out about as well as it turned the wind. We'd caught some of the kids three or four times, but most of them had gotten past us much easier. As soon as we turned our backs, there were kids coming through the fence. Springfield was a tribal cop up on Crow [the Crow Reservation] back then and somebody sent him to help us. The first two kids he caught were about ten or eleven years old. Bob grabbed them by the napes of their necks, one in each hand, and pitched them back over the fence with an admonition that he truly hoped, for their sake, he didn't catch them again. Word passed up and down the fence line pretty quickly and within ten or fifteen minutes we really didn't have anything to do but drink coffee and visit. Not another kid tried to come through the fence that night."

I knew the story was no exaggeration. I met Bob years before down at Fort Washakie and kept track of him ever since. He helped me tremendously when I was putting together a video dictionary of Indian sign language. His fluency in sign language came from learning it as a child seventy-odd years ago while he was learning Arapaho from his grandparents. Using it as a tribal policeman kept him sharp. When Bob started working as a tribal law officer, many of the old-timers didn't speak English. He was rodeoing during the summers and working as a cop in the winter. That meant that he went to whatever reservation needed his services. Sign language allowed him to talk to everyone.

It was while we were working on the dictionary that I'd seen Bob was stout enough to throw kids over a fence. I had gone to his house in Hardin to see him on some business about the dictionary. As I was walking up to the house from the shade where I'd parked my pickup, I noticed him out back working on his car. I realized he was reaching for the battery that was sitting on a bench next to a charger. He was reaching back with one hand, feeling for the battery, so I started to run to help him. I figured an old man like Bob—he was in his late seventies then—would need help. Before I got there, his hand touched the battery, felt around for a grip, then grasped it, lifted it, and put it in place under the hood of his car. I stopped running. Very few middleweights have a hand span big enough to straddle a car battery. Fewer still have the strength to lift one with one hand while their arm is at full extension. Even fewer have the grip to do it with nothing more than a finger squeeze. I can't think of any who could still do it in their late seventies.

It was about three years later when I ran into Bob again. It was at the cafe next to the Little Bighorn Battlefield. I needed a ride back to Sheridan from Crow Agency and stopped in there to see if I recognized anyone who might be headed that way. Bob was just finishing a cup of coffee and allowed that he'd be happy to give me a ride. As we drove, he explained that he was on his way to Lander to launch a personal protest with the Old-Timers Rodeo Committee there. He'd sent in his entry fees for several events and the committee had returned all of them except for team roping. Bob couldn't understand why they had scratched him from bronc and bull riding just because he was eighty-two. He figured if he showed up in person, he could show them that he not only had his strength yet but that he had far more experience than most of the competitors.

You might think that someone that strong, that confident, who was also a boxer, a bronc rider, and a cop, probably wasn't afraid of too many things. But one day when I ran into Bob in Sheridan and offered to buy him a cup of coffee, we adjourned to the Ritz and he told me of one incident when he was fully willing to admit that he was scared.

Back in the twenties and thirties, Bob had worked off and on for a rancher named French, down around Riverton. One of the big chores every spring for anyone who runs a lot of sheep—and Mr. French ran a lot of sheep—is to get the wool to market. Back in those days that trip to town generally involved two or three days with a wagon outfit loaded down with wool sacks. But times were changing in the twenties. Not long after the close of World War I, Mr. French purchased a White truck of some several tons capacity. So it was that one spring when Bob was working for him Mr. French decided that using the truck he could get all his wool into town in one day, even if he had to make a couple or three trips. This is the story Bob told me about the first one.

"We had breakfast before sunup and took off for town. We'd loaded that old White the night before—pretty near half the wool, enough to settle it down on its springs so much I worried some about getting across the draws between the ranch and town. But Old Man French wasn't in too big a hurry. We took it pretty slow and didn't have any problems. Until we got to Riverton, anyhow.

"You know how, coming in from Kinnear, the highway drops off the hills down into town. Well, the old road didn't come in sloping down across the hills like it does now. Back then the road just ran up to the edge of the hills and then dropped off into town. Now, remember, trucks that size were new back then. What driving people had done was in cars and one of the rules of driving cars out here in those days was to be careful of your gasoline because filling stations weren't any too plentiful. That's why everybody was in the habit of shutting off their engines and coasting down the hills. You'd kill the engine, push the clutch in, and let the car roll. Once you'd hit level ground and the car had slowed down a good bit, you'd let the clutch out and the engine would fire back up and off you'd go again. It saved gas and, on some of these hills around here, you could go a whole lot faster than the engine would get you going. I know Mr. French coasted into Riverton every time he drove his car into town. Still, when he killed the engine and started to coast down the hill into Riverton that day, I was a little bit surprised. As heavy as that truck was with all that wool on it, it started picking up speed quite a bit faster than a Model T would have. When the tires squealed as we went around one of the turns, I suggested to Mr. French that he might think about applying a little brake. He replied that he'd burned them out in the turn before that one.

"When I realized that we were in a sure-'nough, honest-to-God runaway truck, and that we were going too fast to jump out without breaking our necks, I did what anyone with any sense would do. The gearshift lever rose out of a big box that stood up above the floorboards, so I dropped down to the floorboards, wrapped myself around that box, and hung on for dear life. Well, you know how the road finally levels out, out there at the edge of town where the college is now. We were pretty nearly flying by the time we got that far, but the road did straighten out and by the time we got along in there where the high school is we'd slowed down enough that I unwound myself from around that transmission case and peeked up over the dashboard again. Just as I did, we dropped off that bench and headed down Main Street. As I looked down at the foot of the hill, where the railroad spur crossed the street, all I could see was a boxcar crossing the street right in front of us. I ducked back down to the transmission case and worked on remembering all the prayers I'd ever known. When the truck slowed down again, down near the foot of Main Street, I decided that either the prayers had worked or that they were switching and there was only that one car. Someone who saw the whole thing from the sidewalk said we missed the boxcar by a good two or even three inches. When I asked old man French about it, he pleaded ignorance about what happened. He said his eyes were shut tight during that part of the ride. Anyhow, when I looked up again, we were just about at the end of Main Street. We left the street down there at the T where Main Street hits the Lander highway, where the park is now. Back then it was just a big field of sagebrush and we plowed up a hundred yards or so of it before we finally came to a stop.

"I gradually unwrapped myself from the gearbox and peeked out. When I looked back up the street, I noticed that there was quite a crowd strung out along the sidewalks looking down the street at us. I looked around at Mr. French and saw that he was still sitting there, his hands wrapped around the wheel so tightly that the color was gone, not just from his knuckles but from his hands clear up to the wrists. Finally, he looked around at me and said, 'Bob, can you drive?' When I tried to answer, I found my mouth was too dry to talk, so I just nodded. 'Good,' old man French said. 'You deliver the wool and then take this truck by the garage and have them fix the brakes. I'm going to walk home.' He had a house there in Riverton and he climbed out of that truck and walked home. Of course that truck was geared so low that there in town it wasn't any trouble to drive it without any brakes. I delivered the wool and then took the truck down to the garage. It took them a couple of days to fix it. When it was ready, I asked Mr. French if he wanted to ride back out to the ranch with me. He said he didn't, so I went back to the ranch, we loaded the rest of the wool, and I took it to town. When I got to the top of that hill, I put that truck in its lowest gear and I crawled down that hill—one foot on the brake and the other on the gearshift lever, to make sure it didn't jump out of gear.

"You know," Bob finished, "I think old man French went back to using a buggy after that. I'm not sure if he ever drove anymore, even his car. Maybe he was as scared as I was. If he was, he was plenty scared."

I still run into Bob every now and again. And every time I do, he has a new story or two. He's had the type of life that makes for good reminiscences, and he knows how to string them into a story.

The Ritz is full of people like Bob, people whose personal memories make good stories. Storytellers, though, are more than folks who have lived a life of stories: They are artists.

Curly Witzel, perhaps the best of the Ritz's storytellers—at least in the eighteen years I've been listening—was such an artist. Curly was also a cowboy of the twentieth century. If Jack Davis was a refugee from the last century's horse-and-buggy days, Curly had fully and completely embraced the modern world.

I don't really remember meeting Curly. He was one of the folks who came in to drink coffee and tell lies at the Ritz most mornings. I gradually became aware that not only was he well liked but most people were willing to listen to him repeat a story they already knew; that's a mark of a good storyteller. I was visiting with Herb Zingg one morning when Curly came in. Herb greeted him with a comment about having heard that he'd been sick. "Yes," Curly replied. "I left the window open the other night and in flew inza." As a dedicated and much abused punster (but then abuse seems to go hand in glove with punning), I was hooked by the line, and by his blue eyes; they were the sort of eyes that were constantly hunting mischief to get into. He sat down next to Herb and I was lost in his stories for the rest of that and many other mornings.

When he was eighty, Curly retired and moved into town,

so his son, John, could attend junior high school; the country school John had been attending only went through the sixth grade. If you do the math required to figure out how old John was then and subtract that from eighty, you'll probably believe any story you hear about Curly, and they're all true. For, you see, Curly made up the world to suit his needs every morning and then slipped it on. It fit surprisingly well for eighty-odd years. He saw possibilities in everything and understood at some deep, intuitive level that each day was a story and he was the author. If the story didn't work out right, it was his fault. He also had the bone-deep under-standing of a true storyteller that history runs in both direc-tions and some things simply haven't had a chance to happen yet. It's all right to include those parts in the story because they'll get around to happening someday and be-come part of the story. If you don't use them, someone else, someday, will; and he'll probably credit you with telling it that way, anyhow. If all of Curly's tales weren't necessarily factual, they all could have been.

As a child, Curly attended a little one-room country school. Toward the end of summer vacation, when he was about ten or twelve, he noticed that a skunk had taken up residence under the schoolhouse. Enlisting the help of two or three of his friends, Curly set about carefully plugging all the holes in the stone foundation except the one the skunk was using as a door. The day before school was to start, all was ready. The other boys stood, rocks ready to plug the last hole, as Curly pulled from the to'e sack he'd brought with him a fox terrier that, as he put it, enjoyed a good fight and didn't have much of a nose. Curly shoved the dog through the hole, the boys quickly plugged it with the rocks, and they all retired to a safe distance for a reason-able wait. When they returned and removed the rocks from the hole, the dog and the skunk were both ready to leave and the school was uninhabitable for a couple of weeks. Curly was pretty popular with all the kids because of the two-week extension of summer vacation.

"Of course," Curly ended the story, "the same kids pretty nearly beat me to death the next spring when the school year ran two weeks longer than it should have, to make up for the late start."

Many people—perhaps most—would have considered this a good lesson, fairly if rudely taught, about the inadvisability of pulling practical jokes. Not so Curly. To Curly, it was a lesson of the price of practical jokes. The price of creating stories by living them is that lumps and bumps come with the stories. Curly certainly was intelligent enough to recognize the lumps and bumps as they came, but he was dedicated enough to his life—to his art, if you will—to accept whatever came with the stories.

Curly developed, as would be expected of an athletic person in rural Montana and Wyoming of those days, into quite a cowboy. Among other outfits he worked for the PK, Eatons', the Padlock, and the Burns ranches. He also rodeoed a good bit, worked first as a stuntman and then as a star in one-reel silent movies, and he did some work for the Burns folks as a stock detective. He'd spent the war as a civilian flight instructor for the army and the navy, and he helped to start one of Wyoming's first air charter services. In other words Curly had lived a life made to order for a story maker, taking advantage of all the things that came his way to make life interesting.

Practical jokes are a great source of stories; Curly knew it and could plan and execute a good one. But he was also quick enough to respond to someone else's prank. He was still just a big kid, maybe fourteen or so, when he was work-

ing on a threshing crew up near Rapeljae, Montana. Curly
was something of a mechanic, so he wound up running the
steam engine on the thresher. He told me that work was
going pretty well except that one kid, a few years older
than him, kept harassing him. Now, those old steam engines
required a lot of active management to keep them operating
properly, so Curly wasn't just standing around.

"The kid was driving a wagon and every time he would
come past me, he'd do something. There was a grease bucket
hanging on the rig. It had a paddle in it that you could slap
grease on things with. If I wasn't watching out when that
kid came by, he'd reach in, grab the paddle, and smear
grease on something. I'd reach down to grab the handle on
a lever and come up with a handful of grease. Finally, he
put a pretty good sized gob of grease on my pants, right
back of my knee, and I decided I'd had enough. The next
time he came by I was laying for him. That old engine had
a release valve on it, so, as soon as his team came alongside the engine, I hit the release and shot a big jet of steam
out in those horses' faces.

"Now, you have to understand that the thresher was set
up at the edge of a wheat field that was better than a quarter
section. There were two horse-drawn mowers cutting the
wheat and at least a couple of dozen men shocking and
stacking it. There were about that many more pitching the
shocks onto the wagons, a half a dozen or so that, when
they were piled high with wheat shocks, hauled the shocks
to the thresher. The crew there would unload it and run it
through the thresher. The finished wheat, all sacked up, was
loaded on still other wagons and hauled to town. When I
blew steam in those horses' faces, they forgot any training
they might have had. They crisscrossed that field three or
four times, scattering wheat shocks and field hands in every

direction. There were guys running every which a way, and the rest of the drivers were doing their dead-level best to keep their teams from joining in the fun. The kid managed to hang on but, for all the effect he was having on the horses, he may as well have jumped off at the start. By the time those two horses had run themselves out he was spent, the crew was scattered, and his last load was spread all over the field. I'm not sure if we ever did find all the pitchforks we'd started with that morning. The beauty of it was that no one except the kid had seen what I'd done, and he was in no position to do anything. And I guarantee that he stopped putting grease on things after that."

Curly may have been a competent mechanic, but he wasn't a farmer. As soon as he was old enough to take off, he quit farming, came down to Wyoming, and went to work cowboying full time. The first year he was in the Sheridan country he worked for the PK, but while he was with them he became acquainted with the Eatons. The next year he went to work for them. Curly was with the Eatons, off and on, for seventeen years, working horses, wrangling dudes, running pack trips, and rodeoing. Bill Eaton was one of the brothers running the ranch during Curly's time there. He once said that having Curly work for him was the same as having four good men quit, since he had to keep an eye on Curly all the time to keep him from pulling too many practical jokes. Of course watching him just made Curly that much more devious. Along the tail end of one winter Curly was in a crew cutting ice for the ranch. (Now, for those of you too young to remember the world without electricity, back then, if you wanted ice in the summer, you had to put it up in the winter. The easiest way, and the one the Eatons used, was to cut blocks out of a frozen pond, stack them in a well-insulated icehouse, and save them for the summer.

A dude ranch like Eatons' went through quite a bit of ice during the summer, so putting up an adequate supply was a major task.) The ice was cut in hundred-pound blocks with saws designed just for ice. Tongs attached to a cable were hooked to the blocks of ice and they were hauled up a ramp to the truck that carried them to the icehouse. Open water increased with the removal of more and more blocks. Balancing on large floating slabs of ice, men used long poles to shepherd the blocks over to the ramp.

Bill Eaton—called Big Bill because he was six foot five or six and heavy framed—was in charge of the crew. Curly was working at the top of the ramp, unhooking the blocks for the crew stacking them on the truck. Big Bill, on an ice slab at the foot of the ramp supervising the operation, announced that they were calling it a day. In checking to make sure that everyone had heard him and was coming in he made two mistakes. First, he let his ice slab drift in front of the ramp. Second, he turned his back on Curly.

"I just unhooked the block just before it got to the top of the ramp," Curly told me. "Then I waited until it was about three-quarters of the way back down before I hollered a warning at Big Bill. He turned around just in time to catch that block of ice. As big as he was, he might have could held it, except that he was standing on wet ice. That block of ice just carried him out into the open water. They made quite splash. Of course there were plenty of fellows standing around with poles to help him back onto the ice. I reckon he'd have killed me except the temperature was down around zero and he was freezing up too fast to chase me. By the time we got him back to the ranch his clothes had frozen up solid and we had to unload him like one of the blocks of ice. I don't know why he figured it wasn't an accident, except maybe that I was involved, but I laid low for a few days until he, well, cooled off might not be the best choice of words, but you know what I mean."

Indeed, I did know what Curly meant. I'd heard enough stories about little incidents of Curly and Bill—things like Curly waiting for Bill to bend over on the offside of a horse and then throwing a saddle with heavy metal stirrups onto the horse's back so that the descending chunk of metal would hit Bill (in the head, as it turns out); or of Curly laughing and asking Bill if it hurt when a broken hondo sent a rope flying back across his face, raising a welt—that I wondered about why he didn't just send Curly down the road. But I knew. People like Curly, who understand and love both horses and people, are rare. To have someone like him around a dude outfit like Eatons' was worth a lot of aggravation. Of course at the heart of it was the fact that Bill and Curly genuinely liked and respected each other. The truth is it's not much fun to pull practical jokes on people you don't like and get along with. But Curly, like all of us, was not immune to Robert Burns's observation about the best-laid plans. As was generally the case in these sessions, Curly and I were having coffee at the Ritz one morning when the topic of practical jokes came up.

"What I thought would be the best joke I ever pulled on Bill turned out not quite like I'd planned it," Curly said. "I was in town picking up the last few things I needed for a pack trip I was taking out the next day. After I had everything I needed, I had to wait a little while until everybody else was ready to go back out to the place, so I stopped by Ernst's Saddle Shop to visit. They'd just finished building a saddle for Big Bill, and naturally they showed it to me. It was beautiful, as Ernst's saddles tended to be, but it was also the first saddle I'd seen with a padded seat. I kept looking at it after the rest of the gawkers had moved away to express their opinions on bits and spurs and such. The seat was deep foam, covered with a beautiful piece of suede leather. I kept thinking about what it would be like to ride on a sponge. As I thought about a sponge, for some reason I thought about the horse liniment I had bought to take along on the pack trip. As I thought about those two things, I just naturally thought about the syringe and needles I'd picked up for doctoring some sick horses out at the ranch. When I looked around, I was alone. It didn't take more than a minute to fill a syringe with liniment and carefully poke the needle through the suede in several places and soak the foam padding with about an ounce of liquid fire. I put my tools away quickly and went back out onto the street to locate the rest of my crowd, so we could get back to the ranch in time for supper.

"When I got back from my pack trip two weeks later and was putting saddles and tack away, I noticed that Bill's new saddle was sitting on its rack. I also noticed that the beautiful piece of suede had been cut off with a pocketknife and that the foam was missing, leaving the rawhide-covered tree exposed. As I was headed back up to the house, I ran into Bill going the same direction. 'What happened to your new saddle?' I asked him, all innocentlike, ready for a good laugh. 'Curly,' he says to me, 'I must have been allergic to whatever they used to tan that suede. I took out an all-day ride the first day I had that saddle and by the time we got back I was so blistered that I had to spend a week in bed, belly down, before I could get dressed let alone try to ride.' I decided that maybe I wouldn't say anything about Bill's allergy, not just then, anyhow."

Generally, Curly's practical jokes worked out a little better, even when they were in response to one pulled on him. For instance, Eatons' has a winter place on Wild Horse

Creek, just down below where I live, to winter their horses. Back one winter when Curly wasn't working for Eatons' but Reed Katchall was, Curly had gone out to Wild Horse to visit for a few days. He told me about what happened.

"I'd been around town too much one fall, working out at the airport. I just needed some time out in the Breaks. I was out there a week or so, riding with Reed every day, getting back into the rhythm of life. The day before I needed to leave, we went up to Arvada for a turkey shoot. I hadn't planned on shooting, but after I saw how few good shots were there and how big the prize tom was, I borrowed a rifle and went down by the river to check the sights. Once I'as satisfied with them, I went back up and entered the shoot. I won that big twenty-pound tom turkey. I was tickled to death because it was only a couple of weeks 'til Thanksgiving and I figured to present my sister-in-law with that bird when I joined my brother and her for Thanksgiving. It wouldn't feed everybody who was coming, but it'd help. We went back to the ranch with the tom in a to'e sack in the back of the pickup. While Reed went in to fix supper, I took the turkey out of the sack and stuck him in the barn for the night. The door didn't have a latch but was dragging so much it took a lot of tugging to get it open and quite a bit of pushing to close it.

"The next morning when I went out to get the turkey, I found the barn door open and the tom missing. When I went back into the house to ask Reed if he had any knowledge of where the bird might be, he said that a big old tom like that had probably pushed the door open with his breast and taken off. I knew it'd take a tom—or maybe a Reed—weighing closer to two hundred pounds than twenty to push that door open. I also knew Reed had a half dozen turkey hens and that he might just be looking for a tom to go with them. But I didn't say anything, I just left like I'd planned to.

"A couple of nights later when I knew Reed would be gone, I went back out to the ranch. Sure enough, there was *my* tom sleeping up on the crossbar over the corral gate with all six of Reed's turkey hens. It just so happened that I had seven to'e sacks and cords with me. I parked my pickup under the crossbar, climbed up on top of the cab, and caught the turkeys. That's pretty easy: They sleep with their heads under their wings, so if you're quick and quiet, you can catch them one at a time, slip them into to'e sacks, and tie the ends off. Then I drove off without leaving any sign of my having been there.

"I took all seven turkeys to my sister-in-law, told her to fix them for Thanksgiving dinner and to save the feathers and the bones for me. She knew me well enough not to ask any questions; she just accepted the birds and saved the remains. When I got them back, a week or two after Thanksgiving, I stuffed all the bones and feathers, along with several pretty good sized rocks to add a little weight, in a box and sent them back to Reed. C.O.D."

Curly did have a bit of the fiddle-foot when he was young; he liked to see new country and try new things. But I've often wondered if moving around a good bit isn't safer for a practical joker. When it came to Hollywood, though, Curly only fled in one direction—he got invited to go there.

Eatons' was the oldest, the largest, and certainly one of the best dude ranches during Curly's heyday. Its clientele was prominent and cosmopolitan, including many from Hollywood. Every Saturday Eatons' had a rodeo where Curly was one of the featured bronc riders. One of the guests, a Hollywood producer, watched Curly ride broncs and watched him handle people. The producer noticed

Curly's head of dark curly hair, his good looks, and what the producer would no doubt have described as his "dashing horsemanship." So he invited Curly out to Hollywood for a crack at the movies. Curly went. He had worked for several years as both a stuntman and an actor and had been the star of four movies when a debate with his producer cut his career short. I asked him about it one morning at the Ritz.

"Well, we hadn't been getting along too well for some time," Curly said. "I'd told him what I thought about his taking advantage of young girls. I mean, he really did have a casting couch. So when he changed directors for my next film, I figured it was to get back at me. The director I'd been working with was really good and we both thought we were going places in the business. I went to talk to the producer about it. Well, one thing led to another and we got to calling one another names and then he reached across the table and slapped me." Curly paused then, as though he were recalling the incident. Where we come from, a slap is not something to be taken lightly; it is both insult and invitation. When he picked up the story again, I knew Hollywood hadn't changed him: Curly was still a cowboy.

"I hit him with a chair," Curly said with an almost embarrassed grin, adding, "Well, he had a couple of his henchmen there and his bodyguard, so we had a pretty good little donnybrook, and when I realized I was the only one still standing in the room I figured I'd better make myself scarce around there. I ran into Hoot Gibson in the hall and we headed back over to my boardinghouse where the landlady hid me in her closet while Hoot went back to the studio and got me a disguise out of the costume department. By the time he got back the cops had already been there. My landlady had let them search my room and then threw them off the scent with a story about my having a girlfriend and why didn't they try looking over where she lived. She even gave them an address off the top of her head. Hoot returned with a policeman's uniform for me. I got all geared up in it and we went to the train station. Hoot just walked up to the ticket window and asked when the next train was leaving. When the ticket agent said in about five minutes, Hoot emptied his pocket on the counter and said, 'Give me a one-way ticket that far.' He slipped me the ticket and I got on the train with several other cops who were all searching for me. They got off when the train started to pull out, I didn't. The ticket got me to Butte, Montana. I wired Hoot when I got there; he hadn't even looked to see where he was sending me. It took five days for me to get it, but he shipped me my trunk with all my clothes, my saddle, and other gear. I didn't go back to California for several years, and I never went back to Hollywood."

I'd had enough association out in that neck of the woods to be curious about what Curly's experiences had been like, fifty years before mine. So for several mornings I pumped him for stories about his adventures in Tinseltown.

"When we were making *Whirlwind Driver*," Curly started in one morning, "we had a scene where we had a fight on top of a stagecoach going full speed. I was driving the coach and one of the stuntmen, playing an outlaw, ran his horse up alongside and jumped onto the coach. I dropped the reins to another driver, hidden down in the boot under my feet, so the horses would stay on the road and keep their speed steady. There was a camera car driving along beside us filming, so the stuntman and I squared off and staged a fistfight. It was easy back then; since the movies were silent, we could set up each punch. You'd tell each other what was coming so that when one guy swung, the other guy could jerk his head back or double up or whatever he needed to do to make it look to the camera like he was being hit. I told him to get ready to take a right to the head and then, just as I swung, the coach hit a bump and rocked him into my fist. I knocked him clear off the back of the coach. I jumped back into the seat and took the reins to stop the coach and go back to see if he was all right. As I got the reins back, the director, who I'd completely forgotten about, yelled, 'Cut!' When I got the horses stopped, I looked back and saw the stuntman coming, unhurt but furious. He thought I'd hit him on purpose. But the director was so excited, he thought the scene was so wonderful, that he offered us each ten dollars extra for the fight scene. When I let the stuntman have my share, he calmed down considerably."

I know enough about stunt work to know that today scenes are choreographed and worked out in great detail to make stunt work as safe as possible. Still, folks get hurt. After listening to the above story, I asked Curly what the accident rate was like back then.

"You know," he said, "surprisingly few of us got hurt. It wasn't any worse than rodeoing. Sometimes even when somebody should have been killed, they got out of it with just bruises. Now, I never did any stunts but horseback ones, but I had this friend who did it all—horses, cars, airplanes, motorcycles; you name it, he'd do it. I asked him one time if he'd ever gotten hurt bad. I'd just watched him do a motorcycle stunt that was pretty impressive and I was amazed he could do things like that and not have some scars to show for it.

" 'Curly,' he told me, 'I never have been hurt bad doing a stunt. But I like to have killed myself going home one night. We'd been shooting up in the Hollywood Hills for a week and every evening as I was heading home I'd had a run-in with two motorcycle cops. They had chased me for speeding every time they'd seen me. I had an Indian bike back then and it had been worked over by professionals. Between that bike and my riding they'd never gotten close to me. Friday we finished the shoot and I figured it would be the last time I'd get to play with those two cops for a while. I was way up at the top of the switchbacks coming down out of the Hills and it was just getting dark enough to turn your lights on when I saw them down at the bottom. They were on their way up and already had their lights on. I hadn't turned mine on yet, and I saw a great joke. I'd leave my lights off and go between them as fast as I could. I figured if I timed it right, I could catch them about midway on one of the straightaways and be gone before they got over their scare and could turn around. I eased along pretty slowly, waiting for them, until I saw their headlights side-by-side just below the next bend. I opened the old Indian up then and came screaming around a switchback and gunned it right between those two headlights.

" 'Curly,' he said, 'do you know how far apart they put the headlights on a Pierce Arrow?

" 'I'd have swore it was those two cops. The only thing I could figure was that the car was somewhere between us when I spotted them and it didn't have its headlights on yet. Anyway, I don't really remember what happened. The next thing I remember was waking up, lying on my back in the top of some chaparral ten or twelve feet off the ground. I felt like I'd been run over by a lot of somethings that were very heavy, but other than a rip in the leather pilot's helmet I was wearing and a few new dings in my leather jacket I didn't seem hurt. I climbed down from the chaparral and wormed my way through it back to the road. There was nobody there: no car, no motorcycle, no cops, no nothing. I hoofed it down the hill for a mile or so and then caught a ride. By the time I got home it was starting to get light; I'd had a good night's sleep up in the chaparral. I called the police right away and reported my bike stolen.

" 'When I finally figured out what had happened, I really regretted being unconscious during most of the fun. The two cops, of course, arrived on the scene a few seconds after the wreck and, I found out later, called in more cops to help look for me. Since they were looking on the ground, they didn't find me and finally gave up and decided to come back and search for my body in the morning. A tow truck came for the car, with my bike attached to it—embedded in it—and everyone went to wherever they were going.

" 'The next day there was nothing the two cops could do. They knew I'd been driving the bike and was trying to get their goats, but they couldn't do anything. Since I had reported the bike stolen, they couldn't say anything about knowing better because they hadn't told anyone about chasing me every night that week; they were embarrassed about not being able to catch me. Besides, everyone figured whoever was on the bike would have been hurt, probably bad enough to have to go to a hospital. So I got away with it. Except, of course, that I lost my motorcycle. And I got a reminder to plan stunts before I tried them. I just wish I hadn't been knocked out. I mean, one second that fellow's driving along without a care in the world and the next he's got an Indian motorcycle buried in the front of his Pierce Arrow and a vision of me removing his windshield and ragtop. Ye gods, I'd have loved to have seen the look on his face as I was passing through.'

"The look in his eyes when he said that is what separated stuntmen like him from stuntmen like me," Curly finished.

"I really think he'd have done that again if he thought he'd been able to see that driver's face as he went by."

I listened to Curly's Hollywood tales with relish. Aside from being a film buff, I'd made a few independent films, tried my hand at scriptwriting, and done research for a couple of directors. Doing research teaches you where to look for things. Curly's movie career fascinated me. My contacts in Hollywood told me that none of his films survived out there. So the next time I had to go back to D.C. I had Curly filed in the back of my head.

One afternoon when I'd finished up what I had on tap at the Library of Congress, I stopped by its film section. Lo and behold, while rummaging through the card catalogue, I found one of Curly's movies, *When Bonita Rode*. I asked to see it and was told that it would have to be brought into the library from the film archives storage out of town. I made an appointment to come by and see it in a couple of days. When I returned, there was a different woman at the desk. She looked up at me as I came through the door and said, "You must be here to see Curly's movie." I'd already noticed that there was something about the way I dress that tipped off people in D.C. that I was from out west, but that she would be aware of Curly was a puzzlement. Then she explained that she had grown up in Sheridan and that her folks lived right around the corner from him. She took me to a viewing carrel, set the film up, and instructed me to leave it set up when I was done, so she could watch it during her lunch break.

When Bonita Rode, it turned out, was a fairly predictable one-reeler. But to see Curly as a young man, to see him as a superb horseman, to watch him leap on his horse and race down a hill most would be nervous taking at a walk: all that was to breathe life into the stories he had told. When at the end of the movie he kissed the heroine, the twinkle in his eyes as he politely swept his hat between them and the camera was something I recognized; it had not dimmed in those long years. Curly had aged, but he had not changed.

"Didn't you ever go back to Hollywood?" I asked Curly one morning.

"Not really," he replied. "Maybe ten years or so later I was at a rodeo in Bakersfield when Will Rogers showed up. He'd been there just as a spectator, you see, but he came back of the chutes to visit. After a while, he asked where we were headed and we all said we were going to have to find someplace to camp out until the next weekend when there was another big show somewhere in the general area. He told us not to camp out but to come to his place. He said he had just had a pen of steers and calves delivered and we could rope all week. So we did, about half a dozen of us. We put up at his place for a week and spent pretty much all day, every day, roping and working horses. He'd come out and join us for a little bit and rope a few head. There was a little steer that was getting chute wise. He came out for Will and cut back to try to go behind him. It didn't seem to matter any to Will, though; he just dabbed a loop back as easy as you please and picked up the steer's horns like that was a normal way of roping. He was just break-away roping, not jerking 'em, and when he popped the rope off that steer and rode back he had that lopsided grin of his on like he was embarrassed about showing us all how easy it really was. And we were all sitting there thinking how thankful we were that he had gone into the movies and we didn't have to compete against him. The best any of us could have hoped for was second-place money against him; and we were as good a ropers as there were going.

"His place was something. It was about three or four hundred acres, a big house and good outbuildings, a big barn and stable, sheds, the whole works. Plus there was a roping arena, a couple of polo fields, some exercise areas, and riding trails all over the place. It was a few miles outside of town, far enough for me to feel safe. I didn't know how long a memory that producer had or whether he was still around. I didn't want to find out either. I just roped there for a week and left. My time in Hollywood was over.

"It couldn't have been over a year after that when Will Rogers was killed. I never went back. I understand it's a park or something now, all preserved like it was. But the town must have grown out all around it by now."

I assured Curly that the town, if you can call Los Angeles a town, had indeed grown out all around it but that there were still plenty of good horses on the place and on most Sundays they still played polo, even if they weren't still roping.

When Curly bragged on a roper, you knew he was good; Curly was as good a roper as a bronc rider. And he was a good teacher, if a little unorthodox. Don Davies, who started rodeoing with folks like Curly and Paddy Ryan as mentors, told me that Curly would only tell you once what to do. If you didn't follow his advice, he might remind you about it as you lay piled into the dirt of some rodeo arena. Don said you weren't likely to forget a second time when it was pointed out that way. Curly, he assured me, was quite a hand, but one of the things that I'd noticed that Don confirmed was that the strict rules of rodeo didn't give Curly full rein for his sense of humor. Rules, by and large, were meat for Curly's love of practical jokes. For instance:

"Paddy Ryan and I found ourselves entered in a wild cow-milking contest at a rodeo one time," Curly told me. (For those of you who've never been to a wild cow-milking

contest the setup is some variation on this theme. A bunch
of cows are turned loose at one end of the arena and a
bunch of two-people teams are turned loose at the other
end. The team member who is horseback ropes one of the
cows while the one on foot milks it. He is required to get
enough milk in the bottle he carries to cover the bottom and
to run back to the finish line. While he's running, the roper
gets his rope off the cow. The catch is that excited cows
don't give much milk.) "I'as doing the roping that day and
Paddy was milking. Those cows were sure enough wild; I'm
not sure any of them had ever been in a pen before, much
less in one surrounded by several thousand screaming people. We knew we were going to have trouble getting milk
out of any of those cows, so we were trying to figure out
some scheme to get one to give up a little milk when we
needed it. It was time for us to go into the arena and we
still hadn't come up with a plan when one of our buddies
walked up eating a vanilla ice-cream cone. Paddy and I
looked at one another and smiled: We were thinking the
same thing. Paddy reached over and took a big bite of the
ice cream. But he didn't swallow it.

"There were about a dozen teams and about fourteen or
fifteen of those truly wild cows in the arena. When the an-
nouncer fired the pistol to start the event, several thousand
people screamed and those cows blew up like a covey of
quail. There were cows and ropes and milkers all over that
arena. There were a couple of wrecks, nothing serious, when
cows hit ropes between a horse and a roped cow. A couple
of milkers got run over, and one got dragged a little way
when one of the cows made a pass at one of the horses
right after the fellow stepped in a dragging loop. It was
absolute turmoil, but when four cows cut across in front of
me, I managed to dab my rope on one of them and pull her

up pretty short. Paddy dove into her flank and came up in a couple of seconds with milk in our bottle. He did remember to wipe his mouth as he ran for the finish line. While he was running, I bailed off my horse and mugged the cow long enough to slip the rope off her horns. I was riding back to the chutes, coiling my rope and looking to see some sign from Paddy about how we did, when I saw Paddy standing there laughing too hard to say or do anything. One of the judges told me we won, but I couldn't get anything out of Paddy for several more minutes. Every time he'd try to talk, he'd start in to laughing again. When he finally got winded, I calmed him down enough to talk. I asked him what was so funny.

" 'Hell's bells, Curly,' he replied, 'if you'd have looked at something other than the head of that "cow," you'd have noticed that you roped a steer.' "

I guess I should have figured that anyone who could not only milk a steer, but get high butterfat content milk out of it, could do anything; but I wasn't really ready for the next set of stories I got from Curly. I'd heard many of Curly's stories and had begun to assemble, in my mind, a rough outline of his life. I realized there was a gap, so one morning while we drank coffee at the Ritz, I asked the inevitable question of men Curly's age: "What did you do during the War?" His answer took me completely by surprise. "I was a civilian flight instructor."

I knew enough to know that you didn't get to be a flight instructor without some pretty good credentials, so I asked Curly about when he started flying. He told me he'd gotten the bug during World War I. The fascination of the air war hooked him, but when the war ended, he was still too young to join the Army Air Corp. He couldn't give up the fascination, so he took lessons and learned to fly on his own. By the time World War II rolled around Curly had beaucoup hours of flying, had helped to found one of Wyoming's first air charter services, and had become an instructor. At the beginning of the war the Army Air Corp was desperate for pilots. They needed to train hundreds, thousands of young men to fly in order to create the air force necessary to win the war. So they built air bases all over the country, and when it became obvious that there weren't enough instructors in the Air Corp to get the job done, they went looking for civilian instructors. Curly was now too old to be an Air Corp pilot, so he volunteered as an instructor and wound up at the new base in Laramie.

"There was one good thing about our location," Curly said. "The runways were 7,200 feet above sea level, the winds blew 25 miles per hour on a still day, and the mountains around us were higher than some of those planes' ceilings. The only thing those kids were going to run into worse than trying to fly those planes around Laramie was combat. Now, remember, they were still using training planes of plywood and canvas. To get out of there to the east, for instance, they had to fly to canyons north or south of town and work their way through them and then out onto the plains. And the winds in the canyons could be tricky.

"The students had specific tasks to accomplish on each flight, but those were kids even if they were, by act of Congress, officers and gentlemen. They were taking part in a grand adventure, they were saving the world, and they had the wildness to volunteer for hazardous duty. So, naturally, they played games as well as doing what they were told. There were always a few extra minutes to see just what they could do, how much they could get out of one of those crates. I wasn't too surprised by what happened.

"One day the base commander called me in and asked me

what I knew about the Wyoming Hereford Ranch. I told him I knew it was one of the big old ranches in the state and a reputable outfit. He then asked if I thought they would complain without good cause. That wasn't a casual question back then when the war was just getting going good and everyone was full of patriotic spirit. I was beginning to sense that something big was coming, so I told him I thought if they had complained, something was probably wrong.

" 'Well,' he said, dead serious, 'then I think we have a problem. It seems some of our students have been buzzing the crew they have reroofing their barn. They're claiming that some of their workers have almost fallen off as a result and they would like for us to stop it.' I knew how big that barn was and I knew it wasn't a problem that would solve itself by going away in a couple of days. I also knew the commander was not one to use a pocketknife when he had access to an axe. Sure enough, the very next day there was a notice posted on all the bulletin boards in camp that anyone buzzing the roofing crews at the Wyoming Hereford Ranch could expect to find himself holding the rank of private in an infantry platoon on a particularly disease-ridden island somewhere in the South Pacific. Or words to that effect.

"That afternoon, when one of the training flights came in, I noticed that one of the planes didn't taxi in with the rest. It stayed out at the edge of the runway. The pilot had jumped out and was looking at something under one wing. I jumped in a jeep and ran out there to see what the matter was. When I got there, I realized that the pilot was the best kid that had ever come through our little institution. He was a natural pilot with great reflexes and hand-eye coordination. He was always ready to push things a little further than anyone else. And he had the instincts of a fighter pilot; you could see it in his eyes. He was also young enough and innocent enough that he didn't have a clue that he could die. As I crawled under the wing to see what he was looking at, though, I could tell that he was aware he might not be a pilot in the U.S. Army Air Corp. I could see a bulge in the underside of the wing where something heavy was resting against the canvas. Then I noticed a little L-shaped tear in the fabric a few inches in front of the bulge. I reached in through the tear and pulled out a roofing hammer. Chalk would have marked black on that kid's face when he saw it: He was trying to imagine the view from a foxhole rather than a cockpit.

"It took the better part of the evening and the better part of a hard-to-come-by, expensive bottle of whiskey to convince the base commander that we were trying to train aerial killers, not men just qualified to fly over parade routes. I pointed out that the kid was the best pilot either of us had ever seen and to send him to the infantry was not just stupid but, at that stage of the war at least, bordering on criminal. He argued back that if he didn't bounce the kid out, there would never be anything vaguely resembling discipline on the base again. We finally hit on a scheme that satisfied both of us. He bounced the kid out of the program into the sort of limbo the military is so good at. Then we brought him back from the dead in the next class with the understanding that if he said anything to anyone about this, he would indeed find himself in the infantry. He believed us. He kept his mouth shut and his flying within the regulations during the next cycle and we sent the Air Corp a potentially great pilot. I always wondered what happened to him."

Talk of the war spread over several mornings. And it led to talk about flying in general. One morning at the Ritz, when the talk ran to antelope hunting and the old-timers were remembering how much better June antelope was than hunting-season antelope, I saw the lights begin to twinkle in Curly's eyes. When the conversation had drifted on to other topics and the center had shifted away from us, I asked him what he had been remembering.

"Back in the early sixties, I had a little Piper Super Cub," Curly started. "It was quite a little plane and I figured I could do just about anything I wanted with it. So one day when I was flying from Cheyenne back up here, I decided I'd see if I could land on top of one of the Pumpkin Buttes." (The Pumpkin Buttes are a major landmark of the Powder River Basin, standing just east of the river where the Bozeman Trail crossed it. Their flat tops are several hundred feet above the surrounding plains.) "I circled them and decided that I could make it on North Pumpkin, so I turned into the wind and set the little Super Cub down. There was more than enough room and it was plenty smooth enough for the gear on that plane. I'd been sitting there for a while, feeling proud of myself and enjoying the view, when I noticed that a bunch of pronghorns were getting curious and walking slowly up to the plane to see what it was. I sat there real still and quiet, and watched to see how close they'd actually get. As they got closer, I noticed that there was a dry doe in the group. The more I watched her, the more I got to thinking about how there certainly weren't any game wardens up there. So as they got right up next to the plane, I reached into the back, very slowly and carefully so as not to excite them, got my six-shooter, eased my arm out of the side window, took aim, and dropped the doe. I cleaned her, wrapped her in a tarp I had with me, and loaded her behind my seat. I flew on up here, thinking about who I'd invite out to the place to share in a little of my good luck.

"There were game wardens all over the airport when I landed. If I'd had enough gas to go anywhere else, I'd have taxied back out and gone somewhere else. Then as I got closer, I realized that none of them seemed to be paying any attention to me. I didn't go right up to the hangar where they were standing though. I stopped a little ways off and walked over there. I got to talking with one of the local boys and found out that they were all there for a meeting and the last plane was just coming in. I visited with them for the few minutes it took for that plane to land and taxi up. The wardens got out, the whole group was getting ready to leave, and I was preparing to heave a sigh of relief when one of them looked over at my plane and asked me if I knew something was leaking from it.

"I didn't have to look to know it was blood, but I turned and gave a good theatrical stare at it before walking over to the plane. Fortunately, he didn't walk over with me and, in those few yards, I found inspiration. 'It's hydraulic fluid,' I shouted back to him. 'Thanks for spotting it. That could have really caused me some problems.' I don't reckon he ever guessed what kind of problems that leak could have caused me if he'd walked over to the plane with me. It's things like that that cause poachers to have weak hearts. They could have confiscated my plane if they'd caught me. I hadn't thought about it up until then, but I sure did think about it after that. Still, June antelope is tasty."

Curly wasn't just a storyteller, he was a subject for other storytellers. Several people had told me the following story, each claiming it had happened at their hometown. I naturally had to ask Curly about it.

"Well," Curly admitted, "it happened more or less like you heard it. I was flying from here down to Denver. As I got closer, I started picking up radio reports about how planes were stacked up waiting to land. I didn't like that because my oil pressure was a little low and I was worried that if I had to circle Denver for an hour, I wasn't really going to be helping my engine. Besides, flying in circles waiting for my turn to land is not the best way I could think of to spend an afternoon. So when I got into Denver's control area, I radioed the tower that I was coming in on one engine. Boy, did they get excited. The tower gave me a straight-in approach, ahead of everyone else, and kept asking me how I was doing. As I came in and saw the crash trucks parked alongside the runway, I began to suspect that maybe they had overreacted.

"Ten minutes later, I was standing in a room full of people, most of whom were screaming at me. I was getting a little nervous about some of the things they were threatening to do to me, which started with hanging and went downhill from there. The man who everyone there seemed to be deferring to just sat there and watched. That made me more nervous than all the threats. When the rest of them finally ran out of threats or wind, I was never sure which, that fellow motioned me into an office. He closed the door so that there were just the two of us and then introduced himself as an FAA inspector. Nervous no longer covered how I was feeling. He then told me that they'd checked out my story about my oil pressure being low. The fact that it was low would probably mean that I would be allowed to keep my pilot's license. He added that he would personally inform every FAA inspector in the country, though, and if I ever tried a stunt like that, or anything else that deviated from prescribed rules and regulations by so much as a jot, I would not even be able to buy kite string. He then asked if I understood. I just nodded; my throat was too dry to speak. Then he asked if I was flying anymore that day. I shook my head that time. That's when he broke into a grin, pulled open the desk drawer, and took out a bottle of whiskey.

" 'Now, off-the-record, I want to have a drink with the man who just pulled the best practical joke I've ever seen,' he said.

"You see," Curly finished, "I was flying a Cessna 180 that day. A 180 only has one engine."

I spent a good bit of time with Curly, listening to his stories. But there was one that I never did get him to tell me. I even asked him about it directly one day. He just smiled and changed the subject. When Hoot Gibson smuggled him out of Hollywood, Curly went to Butte, Montana. Then it took five days for Hoot to get his trunk to him. Butte in the twenties was roaring more than most places. It was a wide-open and wild mining town, with ranchers, cowboys, and loggers sprinkled in. Curly was there for five days, wearing a police uniform. And he never would tell me what happened. Maybe it's better that way; there should always be a few stories left untold.

Curly was, perhaps, the best of the Ritz's storytellers, and the Ritz has been a favorite collecting place. There I learned the rhythm of small-town life. There the cup of coffee takes the place of whittling. I learned a new pace there and a new way to search for stories—checking license plates. In Wyoming our plates are issued in perpetuity. That means that old families in an area have low numbers. And counties are identified. I started watching license plates at the Ritz to see who was there before I went in. As I began to travel around the state, looking for stories, I realized that the Ritz had taught me another trick. By checking the vehicle license plates at a cafe or coffee shop I could determine whether or not there were old-timers in the place, drinking coffee and telling lies.

I do still check vehicles to see if folks I know are there when I arrive at a collecting place. But, in Wyoming at least, I don't have to prospect for places. There's at least one in every town and each has its own group of storytellers. For instance, at the foot of Gillette Avenue, down by the railroad tracks, there's Lula Belle's. It isn't a big place, a half-dozen tables for four, a counter for about eight, and the Table of Infinite Wisdom, which seats eight with a table for three along the wall to handle spillover. This is the place for stories in Campbell County.

I was in Lula Belle's one day when the talk about shoeing horses led into talk about blacksmiths in general. There was an old smith there that morning who knew as much about the lore of his profession as he did about smithing. I asked him about something I'd long wondered about: why horseshoes were supposed to bring good luck. I knew he was a good smith and a good folklorist; I didn't know until he started talking that he was a blacksmith historian too.

"Blacksmiths have always had to put up with people thinking they are dumb," he started in. "I guess it's like football players today. Most folks figure that if you're that big and strong, you don't have to be very smart. Then they make the jump that if you don't have to be, you aren't. So most people figure blacksmiths are dumb. The truth is that a good smith is both a scientist and an artist. There have been times, like during sword-making periods in Toledo and Japan, when the smiths' secrets were kept on pain of death. And the secrets were amazing. A good smith blends the science of alloying, tempering, shaping, and welding with the art of reading metal in their colors as they heat and cool. Why do you think the forge is set back in a dark corner of a shop? It's so the colors are true. But in spite of all the evidence to the contrary people persist in thinking that blacksmiths are dumb. And that's why horseshoes are lucky.

"You see, when a smith is working hot metal with a hammer and anvil, he works with a slow, majestic rhythm that carries over long distances. A smith was working like that one day when the tune he was playing carried down through the earth until Satan himself heard the music. He didn't know what it was but it was good, so he, of course, disliked it and determined to stop it. He sped up to the surface of the earth and donned a disguise so that he could pass among the people unnoticed. He asked around and found that the music was a smith hammering hot steel, so he made his way to the smithy.

"Old Scratch took one look at the blacksmith's height and the size of his arms and jumped to the conclusion that he must be dumb. Now, dumb people are easy prey for Beelzebub, so he immediately hit on the scheme of claiming a soul, and picking up a new pair of shoes in the process. Old Nick has hooves instead of feet, so the kind of shoes he wears are the kind made by blacksmiths, not cobblers. So he just strolls into the smithy, confident that the smith would be too dumb to recognize him in his disguise. He offers the smith a twenty-dollar gold piece for a pair of shoes.

"Of course the blacksmith only has to take one look at this old boy to realize that it's the Devil himself. And it only takes someone as sharp as the smith a second or two to come up with a plan. He made a fine set of shoes for Lucifer, but when he nailed them on he turned the nails around." (For those of you who haven't shod many horses a horseshoe nail is curved. When it is driven in, the point comes out through the wall of the hoof; then it is folded over and clinched so that it won't slip back out, allowing the shoe to fall off. The nail only goes through the dead part of the hoof. Properly applied, a horseshoe hurts the horse as much as trimming your fingernail hurts you. But, turned around, the curve of the nail drives it into the quick, much like a splinter being driven under your fingernail.) Old Dan Patch is so tough that he didn't notice the nails going in, he just admired the shoes, gave the smith the money, and headed home, knowing that as soon as the smith spent the money his soul would be condemned to Hell.

"The smith had no intention of spending the money; as soon as he was alone, he threw it into the center of the forge and got busy with the bellows until he had melted it down and burned it up. Meanwhile, down the road a few miles the Prince of Darkness was sitting on the side of the road prying his new shoes off with his pocketknife. Though he hadn't felt the pain when the nails were driven in, several miles of walking pretty nearly crippled him. Once he'd gotten the shoes off and sore-footed it home, he found out that he hadn't even gotten the blacksmith's soul. That was enough for him. He decided never to have anything to do with blacksmiths ever again.

"That's why if you find a horseshoe and throw it over your shoulder, it'll protect you. If the Old Boy is following you, planning on doing you some harm, and finds a horseshoe on your path, he'll figure you're a blacksmith and won't want to have anything to do with you. He'll just turn aside.

"Always remember," the old smith finished, "horseshoes are lucky not because the Evil One is scared of them but because he's scared of blacksmiths. We're just too smart for him."

As I listened to the old blacksmith telling a classical folktale, I thought of the amazing variety of stories I've run into around the West. Some, like the smith's tale, are clearly fictional. Other stories are definite maybes, just barely possible or greatly stretched. And then there are those that are not only true but factual.

Cody, Wyoming, is named for Buffalo Bill. The old hotel in town, which Buffalo Bill built, is named for his daughter, Irma. Buffalo Bill liked fine saloons, so he put a fine saloon in the Irma—featuring a $100,000 cherrywood backbar Queen Victoria had given him. The saloon didn't survive Mr. Volstead; now it's the hotel's coffee shop. But it's still an excellent place to collect stories. Of all the stories I've heard there, one does as good a job as can be done of illustrating how complex Buffalo Bill was. The story is clearly fictional, a tall tale if ever there was one. Except that it really did happen. I've heard many people tell it right there at the Irma. Dave Bermingham, a local artist, tells it about as well as anyone. I heard him tell it one morning at the Irma to some visitors.

"It was when the Irma here was new—for that matter when Cody itself was new," Dave started. "They had some sure-'nough good poker games here back then. Buffalo Bill divided his time between his ranch and his business in Cody. One night when Buffalo Bill was in town, there was a particularly high stakes poker game at the Irma. Cody, of course, sat in. Along when it was getting to be a question of whether the players were staying up late or getting up early, someone dealt a fine hand to everyone at the table.

"You know how it is when everyone's holding good cards. They all remember the rule that there's no hand that's only good enough to call with. Everyone kept raising until there was a helluva pot on the table. Buffalo Bill had the last raise, so he had to show his cards first but he didn't.

" 'Gentlemen,' he said, 'I've absolute confidence that I'm holding the winning hand. Since none of you have folded, I assume you are equally sure of your cards. I have a proposal: We are trying to start a town here, one that can grow and prosper. I'm not a particularly religious man, but I know a town can't survive without a church. I suggest that we all throw our cards in, shuffle the deck, and that none of us ever reveals what he was holding. We can then take the money in this pot and build this town a church.'

"I guess they all knew Buffalo Bill was right, because they did it. They threw their hands in, shuffled the deck, and built the church. And not a one of them ever told anyone what he was holding."

The next time you go to Yellowstone via the east gate remember to look, a little ways past the Buffalo Bill Historical Center, on the left. You'll see a beautiful little white frame church. It's the Episcopal Church, but to everyone in Cody it's the Poker Church.

My wanderings over the years have taken me over most of the West and a good deal of country back east. The lessons of listening and of language I learned from Daddy down in Texas and those of collecting stories—how to locate them, how to sort through the chaff to locate the kernels of truth, and other tricks of the trade—I learned at the Ritz seem to be valid everywhere. Not all the stories have a Buffalo Bill in them, but each one is as important to its place as the story of Buffalo Bill and the Poker Church is to Cody. I also understand how important it is to have places for those stories to be told. Much of our history—personal, family, local—is oral; it lives in the telling. These histories are of no use only in a book. To be useful, they must be known, they must be told, they must pass on from one generation to the next.

I had the rare good fortune to be exposed to the best storyteller I've ever known from my earliest memory—I may be biased about Daddy but that's okay, I'm right. With Daddy's help, I developed a love for stories and have had many opportunities to indulge myself. Bill's trailer, Jack's pack

171

shed, the Ritz, a thousand campfires, and countless cafes have given me more chances to collect and learn stories than most folks have. It is important for the stories to be heard in context, as I first heard them. There are places where that still happens. Sam Paul Mavrakis, Sam's son, has returned home to work with his father, so the Ritz will continue for another generation to provide a place for Sheridan's history to be told. I guess Sam Paul makes this chapter superfluous, but maybe you will, over a cup of coffee one morning, tell some of these stories and help keep them alive.

In
Conclusion

❖━❖━❖

On a spring night in 1980 I found myself, through a strange set of circumstances, sitting in a small theater telling stories Bill Daniels had told me. I sat in a rocking chair, lit by a coal oil lamp on the table next to me, spinning out the yarn of Bill's life's tales, when I realized that he was sitting there across the table reminding me of the tales I'd forgotten. By the end of the show I'd discovered my voice and jumped at the chance to go to the Buffalo Bill Historical Center for a couple of weeks as a storyteller during the museum's summer entertainment series. Two weeks led to four; some teachers heard me and I received a couple of invitations to perform at schools and, basically, I've never been fit for honest work since.

So for the last fourteen years I've been working as a storyteller. I spend my time digging up old-timers before they need to be dug up literally, develop the stories I hear into stories I can tell, learning what I can about performance, but mostly just trying to find the rhythms of the traditions the stories grow from so I can understand them and tell them properly. For the last couple of years I've been trying to translate the spoken word language of storytelling into a written form that doesn't butcher the oral style and the context too much.

One of the primary lessons I've learned from collecting stories is that stories generally aren't told in isolation. A theme is established in a session and everyone who has a story on the theme takes a turn. When folks begin swapping stories, I've observed that the first rule of storytelling always applies. Daddy explained the rule to me years ago, quoting Uncle Frate:

"The first liar never has a chance."

INDEX